ANNUITIES & MUTUAL FUNDS

What Every Investor Needs to Know but Hasn't Been Told

by
James McClelland

authorHOUSE™

1663 LIBERTY DRIVE, SUITE 200
BLOOMINGTON, INDIANA 47403
(800) 839-8640
WWW.AUTHORHOUSE.COM

First published by AuthorHouse 07/25/05

ISBN: 1-4208-5929-3 (sc)

Printed in the United States of America
Bloomington, Indiana

This book is printed on acid-free paper.

Table of Contents

Section I – General Investing Knowledge and Strategy 1

Section II – Mutual Funds
    Chapter 1 - History of the Mutual Fund Industry 21
    Chapter 2 - What is a Mutual Fund? 25
    Chapter 3 - Types of Mutual Funds 29
    Chapter 4 - Mutual Funds and What They Cost 35
    Chapter 5 - How Does This Affect Me? 47
    Chapter 6 - Taxes: How they Impact our Decision 55

Section III - Annuities
    Chapter 7 – Introduction 61
    Chapter 8 - The History of Annuities 67
    Chapter 9 - Variable Annuities 73
    Chapter 10 - The Reasons to Purchase a Variable Annuity 79
    Chapter 11 - What Does All This Cost? 109

Section IV - Fixed Annuities 119

Section V - Index Annuities 123

Section VI - The Bottom Line 127
    Notes and Resources 135

Section I – General Investing Knowledge and Strategy

When I first got the idea to write this book, I wanted to produce a body of material that was both informative and easy to follow. The financial world has so many products and services available to you, the average consumer, that it can be mind-boggling to even think about which is appropriate for you. I'm sure that many of you reading this invest in a 401(k) plan, or something similar such as a 403(b) or 457 plan, as well as maybe have an IRA, possibly even several IRAs, and hold individual securities such as stocks or bonds. All of these investments combined would constitute your particular portfolio of investments. I haven't even included in this portfolio the two investment vehicles we're going to cover in this book: mutual funds and variable annuities. That is a vast amount to keep track of and to have a basic understanding of how they work and how they can be beneficial to both you and your family.

Cash flows into mutual funds have continued to increase steadily over the last quarter century, and the total dollar amount now invested in them is in excess of six trillion. I don't know about everybody else, but that is a ton of money to me! So, with that much of our money invested, it certainly stands to reason that we all have a very good understanding of how mutual funds operate and, of course, how to pick the most advantageous ones to invest in.

Right?

Then there is no need for me to keep writing this book.

I thank everyone for taking the time to read my brief introduction, and I wish everyone the best of luck with your C-share funds, with low 12-b1 fees, and hopefully, a short CDSC.

What's that? You said you're not exactly sure what all those terms were that I just used to describe a type of fund that you might consider buying or that you may already own? If that's the case, then I guess I'd better write the rest of this book, and I would strongly suggest that you keep reading so you'll be prepared with a well-grounded understanding of these products when you either go to purchase one or have one being sold to you. Many times, the investment representatives attempting to sell you on a particular mutual fund will dazzle you with performance numbers, showing how much money you would have made had you been invested in that fund for the past three, five, or even ten years. While this information is an important tool in making your ultimate decision, I'm going to arm you with a few other probing questions that will uncover other pertinent information necessary for you to make the proper choice.

Now, that is the mutual fund world, a world that I think most of you have at least heard of and probably are participating in, so you definitely have some working knowledge of mutual funds. The annuity world, on the other hand, seems to have this cloud of mystery surrounding it, with rumors and myths galore on how they operate and whether or not they're suitable investments.

How many of you have heard of annuities in any capacity?

I'm going to guess that a fair percentage of you have, either through an article you might have read, maybe a story you saw on CNBC, or just through a general conversation about how to invest your money. Now, I want to ask you a follow up question:

How many of you feel you have a grasp of how annuities really work?

My guess about your answers on this question is that a very small percentage of you could answer yes. I find it really amazing that so little is known among the common investors about products such as annuities that are generating sales in excess of $200 billion a year! Am I alone on this one, or does that sound kind of odd to anybody else?

I think that the main reason why people don't really know about the properties of annuities is that the people selling the products (i.e., the brokers, investment representatives, or whatever other title they may have) don't truly understand them in the first place. Now, that is a blanket statement, and I don't mean to include all investment representatives because there are some who do understand how the products and their benefits work, but from my experience in this industry and from talking to brokers every day, I can tell you with certainty that the majority of brokers selling these products have no better knowledge of how they work than you do.

This is not a condemnation of all investment representatives because I'm the first person to admit that selling financial products and solutions to customers and being responsible for handling their future financial well-being is an extremely difficult job. Not to mention that the financial world and the regulations governing it are incredibly complex, especially when one considers the different tax ramifications of certain investments. With all that being said, there are many investment representatives who simply don't sell annuities because they either don't want to take the time or can't afford to take the time to learn about them. The representatives who do sell annuities are the ones that I'm referring to.

Annuities can be complex and have several moving parts. Consequently, they are missold. This is part of the problem, but the larger problem is that annuities pay investment representatives lucrative commissions, and that is why they sell them. Learning the products thoroughly is a secondary concern; they simply want to know some basics about them so they can make an effective enough sales pitch, close the deal, and collect the commission. That might seem a bit harsh, but I've seen too many instances where that is precisely the case.

This fact alone shows the vital importance that you, as the consumer, have some basic working knowledge of the product that you are buying. Considering that this investment is dealing with your hard-earned money and is probably money you are counting on at some point in your life, most likely for retirement, then it is one of the most important decisions you will ever make.

My goal is to give you a general working knowledge of annuities and mutual funds so you can internalize the information being presented to you and be able to draw concrete conclusions about which of these investment vehicles would best suit your particular needs. Perhaps neither one is the right choice for you, and it's important that you be able to find that out from the very beginning rather then get involved in an investment and find out at a later date that it was the wrong decision and then have to pay a penalty to correct that mistake.

There are general principles that run throughout annuities and mutual funds, and if you can just have a grasp on these fundamentals, then I have no doubt that you can listen to all the bells and whistles that you will be presented with and determine which, if any, are right for you. If you sit through a presentation to buy an annuity, particularly a variable annuity, you'll hear such phrases as premium bonus, death benefit options, and living benefit riders. These catch phrases are options that insurance companies offer on their variable annuities (VAs) in order to distinguish themselves from one another. You will quickly learn in this book that the VA market is increasingly becoming a game of one-upmanship in which insurance companies feel they must compete in order to win your investment dollars. If a given insurance company adds a new benefit or enhances an existing benefit on one of their products, rest assured that within six months to a year, all of their top competitors will launch essentially the same feature, with a little twist in order to appear unique, on their own products. You will see how this plays out in more detail when we discuss the different options available on VAs.

Recently, in the headlines, you have probably read about scandals within the mutual fund industry, with such firms as Putnam and AIM/Invesco, which are prompting the regulatory agencies that govern them, namely the SEC and NASD, to review their procedures. These scandals dealt specifically with what is known as market timing. Market timing is a technique that some investors use in order to take advantage of temporary shifts in the stock market. For example, an investor might move a large sum of money from one sector of stocks to another sector for a short period of time, as short as a few hours, in order to take advantage of that day's market conditions. Typically, this practice is forbidden in mutual funds because it can have an adverse effect on the returns of the funds in question. The people who might use market timing are usually individual investors with large sums of cash or institutional investors, such as pension funds, who could have several million dollars invested in any given fund. Make no mistake, these are the investors to whom mutual funds cater, and sometimes, they bend the rules in order to keep their assets under management. So, of course, as these scandals were brought to light, the governing bodies and the accused companies quickly went into crisis-control mode. The SEC and NASD announced plans for tighter regulations and severe penalties for these types of actions, and the companies themselves made a few firings and also announced their plans for tighter in-house regulations to prevent this from happening again. My point here is that although you will hear how the financial community is cleaning up the mutual fund industry, there will always be ways around these so-called tougher regulations. Remember that the people running mutual fund companies and handling billions of dollars in assets are very intelligent people! They are some of the brightest in the country, and they get paid accordingly. They will always be a step ahead of the regulations. Again, the majority of mutual funds and mutual fund companies do follow the rules and strongly discourage these kinds of practices, but there will always be a few out there who will turn their heads in the other direction and allow these indiscretions if it means retaining assets and meeting performance figures. That is why it is paramount that we, as common investors, have an understanding of what we are buying and who is managing our money.

How does this apply to annuities? Well, in my opinion, once the fury of these scandals quiets down, the governing bodies will eventually turn their attention to the annuity marketplace. Certain states, namely New York, have already imposed stricter guidelines in their suitability requirements regarding the sale of annuities. These stricter regulations will continue to spread as both states and the federal government take a longer look at the sale of annuities. Again, this by no means assures that you will be protected against being the victim of a fraudulent annuity sale. It also illustrates the importance of the point of knowing what an annuity is, how it operates, and whether or not it fits your particular investment needs.

Investing for retirement has become one of the most important decisions that a person or persons will make in their lives. The advancement of science and medical treatment is so astonishing, and now, with the seemingly limitless possibilities of genetic DNA research and stem cell research, the average person's life expectancy is increasing every year. Knowing that and assuming that the generally accepted retirement age of sixty-five remains constant, that means that people are spending more and more of their lives in retirement. So, now the retirement funds that were amassed during your working career must last even longer than they did just ten or fifteen years ago. If you are in your thirties or forties, for example, and still have twenty or so years to retirement, can you imagine how far medical science will have taken us by then?! If the average life expectancy at this moment is around seventy-eight years old, (I know that this varies from men to women and across different ethnicities, but this is just an average number) that is thirteen years in retirement, assuming we retire at age sixty-five, through which your retirement savings have to last you. Let's make the assumption that we have about twenty years till retirement, and by then, we'll also assume that the average life expectancy has increased to eighty-five years old. That gives us a figure of twenty years of retirement, which means, on average, we'll be retired for about half as long as we were in the work force, assuming we worked for forty years. That certainly seems like a manageable number. Between 401(k) and IRA savings, stocks, bonds, and other investments and perhaps a pension plan if you are a state or government employee, there should be enough funds built up over that time to cover your retirement expenses. That may be true. However, I want to present you with a few figures that may help put into perspective just how much money you and your spouse may need for those twenty years.

I'm going to give you some figures, and then we're going to put them into an equation.

2—Represents you and your spouse
3—Represents three meals a day
365—Number of days in a year
20—Number of years in retirement
$5—Cost of each meal
That gives us the following:

2 x 3 x 365 x 20 x $5=$219,000

That means, for you and your spouse to eat for those twenty years in retirement, it will cost $219,000, averaging just five dollars per meal. I don't know about you, but this fact certainly opened my eyes! And that is just basic survival; it includes no dinners at restaurants, not leaving any tips, and no snacks in between meals. It basically means that eating cheap fast food for your entire retirement will cost you over $200,000! That is a huge expense. It's just one of the expenses that you will face in retirement. Again, I'm going to ask the question:

Do you think that planning for retirement is one of the most important decisions you'll ever make?

The facts I just quoted also don't take into consideration the effects of inflation. Inflation has historically run at about 3%, and, as I'm sure you are aware, can eat away at the purchasing power of your dollar. To illustrate our example even further, $5 at the end of 1983 would be the equivalent of spending $9.24 at the end of 2003. This is nearly double the amount needed to purchase the same goods. So, not only must your retirement funds keep up with living needs, but they must also be able to keep up with the economic inflation over those twenty years as well. You can't afford to lose time by picking the wrong type of investment for your needs. An annuity or mutual fund may very well be the answer for your investment needs, because as I'm going to show, both do have their advantages, but which one is the right one?

I'd like to give you some general knowledge about where to invest your money. There are a lot of myths floating around about whether the stock market is the right place or the bond market or CDs or real estate. Real estate has historically been a terrific investment, and if you have the resources to enter that market, I would highly recommend it, because it has been a great source of wealth accumulation over the years. However, since this book is for the common investor and most common investors that I know of don't have the necessary financial resources to actively participate in the real estate market, we are going to exclude this for the purposes of this discussion.

Leaving the real estate market out of the equation, the stock market is the next choice as to where to invest your money. It has historically far out-paced the bond market, whether it be U.S. Treasury bonds or corporate bonds, CDs, and/or bank savings accounts. I know that the stock market and certain stocks in particular have gone through trying times since March of 2000, when the so-called "dot.com" bubble burst, but the fact remains that a diversified investment in stocks is the best alternative to real estate in order to accumulate wealth and outpace inflation.

Stock prices have dropped significantly over the past four years (from 2000–2004), and there are several reasons for this. Obviously, the tragic events of September 11th, 2001 and the ongoing fear of future terrorist attacks is a major factor, but other events coincided with this to exacerbate and accelerate the market decline. The Enron and Worldcom scandals and the subsequent indictments and trials of their corporate officers have raised serious doubts in the public's mind about the trustworthiness of Corporate America and shaken the confidence held in these organizations. These two factors led into another factor in the stock market decline, which was the decline in corporate profits. This is a big key because corporate earnings and, more importantly, profits are what drive a company's stock price. As corporate profits decline, they reduce spending, put on hiring freezes, and outsource certain jobs to cheaper foreign labor markets, which can lead to layoffs and firings here at home.

Let me make an analogy to the suppressed prices of stocks right now. It's as if you're buying them on sale. What attracts us as consumers to make certain purchases? Well, need is certainly a factor, but invariably, price is a major part of the decision as well. Remember the times we'd ask our mother why she came home with six new packs of underwear for us when you only needed two? The answer is always because they were on sale! So, the need for new underwear was there, as all mothers are concerned that their children all have on clean underwear, but it was also a good buy.

Investments, whether they be stocks, bonds, real estate, etc. also follow the rules of need and price. Everyone needs investments of some sort to provide for them in retirement, and as the old adage says, you want to buy low and sell high. If you've been wavering on a purchasing a certain product, like a new plasma TV, and you suddenly see it on sale with a 30% or 40% discount to its original price, then you would be more inclined to buy it.

With the price that stocks are at now in 2004 and have been at for the last two years or so, they are on sale from the levels of the late nineties. I mean, they have slashed prices! It is almost akin to a furniture store having a clearance sale. All merchandise must go! For an example, let's take a look at the S&P 500 Index. Traditionally, the S&P 500 is an index comprised of 500 companies designed to give an overall sense of the health of the stock market as a whole by showing a composite of all of those companies' stock prices. In March 2000, the S&P 500 Index peaked at just about 1,527, an impressive number that years before many experts thought would not be possible. Life was great for investors during this time. The market did nothing but go up, and everyone was going to be a millionaire within ten years. As we know, it didn't work out that way and many investors, including myself, suffered enormous losses over the following two plus years in both our individual investments as well as in our 401(k) and IRA accounts. That same S&P 500 Index three years later in 2003 was at 895. That's a 41.38% drop. I'd say that is a significant sale. The argument against this line of thinking is that the stocks were greatly overvalued in March 2000, and they just simply corrected back to where their prices should have been. That may be true, but history doesn't bear this out.

Taking a historical look at the stock market since 1929, the year of the famous stock market crash that sent the United States spiraling into the Great Depression, we get some idea of how the market has reacted to sustained periods of decline. That gives us some seventy-four years of market history from which to draw some conclusions. Let me preface this by giving you the same disclaimer that any investment representative or insurance company should give you as well and say that historical returns are by no means a guarantee of future performance. This phrase is stamped on every client-approved marketing piece in which companies make any reference to their past performance, and there is good reason for that. It would certainly be misleading and unethical to simply show you a piece of literature and say, "Our company's product has averaged a 14.8% return every year for the past five years and that is what you can expect in the next five years." Every situation is unique, and if anyone could predict exactly what was going to happen in the next five years, they certainly wouldn't need to be selling you a mutual fund or annuity! That being said, we shouldn't just throw historical data out the window and dismiss it as meaningless either. Remember the old adage "Those who do not learn from history are doomed to repeat it." While history can never be an exact predictor of future occurrences, we can learn a great deal from examining it, and it can aid us in making an informed, intelligent decision regarding our investments.

The S&P 500 Index will be our measuring stick for this experiment since we've already touched on it earlier. In the last seventy-four years, there have been four times when the S&P 500 has had negative returns for at least two consecutive years. The first instance of this occurred from 1929 to 1932, of course, following the stock market crash in October of 1929 and the subsequent depression that we mentioned earlier. During this time, the Index was down 86.1%, the largest percent decline of any of the four time periods we will examine. However, a look at the five years immediately following paints a different picture. The cumulative return of the Index from July 1932 to July 1937 is a positive 254.8%. Now, certainly there were some fluctuations during that five-year period, but if you stayed the course and stayed invested solely in the Index, you would have seen a 254.8% gain. If we do some very basic math, that translates to about a 50% return per year! This is a number I think we would all be quite happy with. The people who benefited from this gain were the ones who had the confidence and foresight to stay the course and invest in the market when these stocks were on sale in 1931 and 1932. I know that is certainly easier said than done since most of the common investors of that period were just looking for any kind of work to support their families and not lose their homes, but when they did get back on their feet, a lot of them were shell-shocked from what had happened. These investors decided to play it safe from then on and either invested their money into savings accounts earning a minuscule rate of return or simply took it and stuffed it under the mattress! Does it take quite a bit of guts and courage to stay the course even when you are taking some losses? You bet it does. When investing in the market for retirement, ten, twenty, or even thirty years down the road, it is the people who stay invested when the market is down and even increase their position when the market is down that reap the benefits over the long-term.

Carrying this example out even further and looking at the following fifteen and twenty-five-year periods reveals even more. The following fifteen years show a cumulative rise of 212.3%. You'll notice that this is actually less then the five-year number of 254.8%. It's still a very respectable return of about 14% per year; however, it also overlapped the next period of decline that we're going to discuss, which was the period during the start of World War II. That certainly helped to pull the fifteen-year number down, but as I said, it was still a respectable increase. The twenty-five-year cumulative rise in the Index, however, is an eye-popping 1008.8%! For all those who are counting, that averages out to just over 40% per year for twenty-five years. I'll reiterate that there certainly would be fluctuations within that twenty-five-year span, but if you stayed the course from 1932 through 1957, then you would have seen your investment in the Index do exceptionally well, and in all likelihood, provide you with the means to retire comfortably. The following chart lays out exactly what we have just discussed in an easier-to-follow format. It also shows all four periods of decline in the Index over the past seventy-four years and the subsequent returns for five, fifteen, and twenty-five years.

Period	Decline	Next 5 yrs	15 yrs	25 yrs
9/6/29 – 7/8/32	-86.1%	+254.8%	+212.3%	+1008.8%
12/30/38– 4/28/42	-43.2%	+92.4%	+512.2%	+1159%
1/11/73– 10/3/74	-48.2%	+75.96%	+1994.7%	+2040.1%
3/24/00– 12/31/02	-43%	Unknown	Unknown	Unknown

As you can see from 3/24/00–12/31/02, the Index was down −43%, very comparable to the two previous sustained declines. So what does this hold for the future? I don't know, and the truth is that no one knows, but I'm confident in saying that if you were to tell investors and investment representatives in 1974 that the Index would rise by over 2000% over the next twenty-five years, you would have won a lot of bets! Does that mean that the S&P 500 will have returns on this scale over the next five, fifteen, and twenty-five-year periods? The answer is no. Nothing in this world is certain except death and taxes, and even taxes are optional depending on how good your accountant is! (That's just a joke in case anybody from the IRS is reading.) We can't say with certainty that we will experience growth on the level that we have in the past, but seventy-four years is a pretty reliable time frame from which to draw some conclusions. I mean, those seventy-four years have seen our country sustain world wars, presidential assassinations, depressions, skyrocketing oil prices, and terrorist attacks. There isn't much that we haven't been through over that time span and in the three previous instances, as the chart lays out, we have recovered economically and enjoyed sustained periods of considerable growth.

My emphasis here is that now is the time to get invested in the market if you're not already, and if you are already invested, continue to stay the course, and if possible, increase your positions. The best way to take advantage of the growth that is likely to occur over the next several years is to hold positions in the stock market; however, holding a diversified position in individual stocks can take quite a bit of money. The best way for common investors to accomplish this is through investment vehicles that pool money together from investors and use professional money managers to invest it. Two popular examples of these vehicles are mutual funds and annuities, particularly variable annuities. Before we talk specifically about either of these vehicles, I wanted to first give you some background as to why it is so important to start planning for retirement and which are the best means to accomplish that goal over a span of years.

I want to wrap up this section with one final set of statistics to show the importance of including stocks in your investment portfolio. This was a study conducted by Trinity University and took into account the relevant market data from 1946 to 1999. The aim of the study was to show which blend of stocks and bonds in an investment portfolio would have the best chance of sustaining a certain income stream over a thirty-year time frame. The allocations between stocks and bonds ranged from 100% stocks all the way to 100% bonds. I think the results may be surprising to some of you, because I know they were to me to an extent.

Income Needed	*100/0%*	*75/25%*	*50/50%*	*25/ 75%*	*0/100%*
9%	56%	44%	12%	4%	0%
8%	80%	64%	36%	4%	4%
7%	100%	100%	84%	16%	12%
6%	100%	100%	100%	96%	20%
5%	100%	100%	100%	100%	56%
4%	100%	100%	100%	100%	100%
3%	100%	100%	100%	100%	100%

Italic numbers—% of stocks held in the portfolio
Bold numbers—% of bonds held in the portfolio

Let's take a look at the first row of numbers[1]. This shows what percentage of the time during that fifty-four-year span from 1946 to 1999 each particular allocation would have been able to sustain a 9% income stream. The first number shows that a portfolio consisting of 100% stocks would have sustained that rate of income 56% of the time during that time frame. So that is just above a 50/50 shot that your retirement dollars, if invested completely in stocks, would have been able to sustain you through a thirty-year retirement. That's certainly not a bad number due to the fact that drawing 9% a year in withdrawals off your investments is a substantial number. You'll also see that if we add just 25% bonds to our portfolio mix then our chances of keeping pace with those withdrawals drops to 44%. You certainly know how to read the chart for yourself by now, so I won't bore you to death by examining every figure, but there are a few that I want to point out to you. During that time frame and having to draw 9% withdrawals off your investments, if you had no stock exposure and were 100% in bonds, you had 0% chance of sustaining that income for thirty years! In essence, you were going broke slowly. You may say, well, 9% is just too high a number, and I would probably never need to draw that much off my investments to live on. I'll grant you that, so let's just take a look at a 7% income stream. The first two columns would have achieved that goal 100%

[1] Source is a 1999 Trinity University study published by Philip Cooley, Carl Hubbard, and Daniel Walz.

of the time. Even increasing the bond exposure to 50% in column 3 would have met our requirement 84% of the time. But again, if we took a very conservative approach and invested 100% in bonds, we only had a 12% chance to meet that income goal. As a betting man, I don't like my odds very much in either of those scenarios. In order to further illustrate the point, let's say, for example, that we have done our homework and saved diligently during our career and have accumulated investment assets, not including your house or other real estate, of $500,000. This is a fairly sizeable nest egg it would seem. It would seem so until we do some math. 7% of $500,000 is $35,000 per year in income. When we look at it in that context, it makes our $500,000 shrink up quite a bit, doesn't it? With the historical average rise in inflation of 3% per year and no other income from a job, $35,000 a year isn't a whole lot of money. Remember, our earlier example of the cost to feed two people through just twenty years of retirement at very basic levels was over $200,000! That works out to $10,000 per year of your $35,000 would go to just food alone! Staying 100% in bonds would only give us a certainty of receiving a 4% income stream. 4% of our $500,000 is a mere $20,000 per year and as we just discussed, half of that, $10,000, would go to purchasing food. That would leave just $10,000 per year to cover the rest of your bills, expenses, and leisure activities. I can't think of anyone I know of who could live comfortably on just $20,000 per year. You could probably survive through retirement on that income, but it certainly would be bare minimal survival. Retirement is a phase in an individual's life that is supposed to be enjoyed and lived in some sense of comfort, not simply just survived. After all, you worked hard for thirty or forty years and deserve to enjoy the time you spend in retirement.

I'm not giving you this information in order to scare you, although it can be a scary prospect to think about, but to share with you the need to have a significant portion of your investments in the stock market and to have a solid fundamental understanding of the investment vehicles that can get you there. Now that you have the background information as to why it is so important to plan for retirement decades in advance, I'd like to talk specifically about two investment choices, mutual funds and annuities, which can help you

reach your goal, and determine if they are even the proper investments for you and your particular situation.

Section II – Mutual Funds

Chapter 1 - History of the Mutual Fund Industry

Our discussion about mutual funds will start with their inception. The first mutual fund in the United States was founded on March 24th, 1924. It was called the Massachusetts Investors' Trust. It was an open-ended mutual fund, which means it could constantly issue new shares to new investors. After its first year of operation, the fund had over 200 shareholders and $392,000 in assets. For some perspective on the growth of the mutual fund industry over the last eighty years, see that at the end of 1924, there were roughly $10 million in assets invested in mutual funds and by the beginning of 2004, there were $6.8 trillion in assets invested in over 10,000 mutual funds! This constitutes a huge sum of investors' dollars and about 83 million individual investors have money in these vehicles in some way or another.

From their introduction in 1924 through the beginning of the 1950s, the growth in the industry was rather slow. We've touched on a few of the reasons for this, the stock market crash of 1929 and the outbreak of World War II, and despite the government's efforts to impose regulations on the industry through the creation of the Securities and Exchange Commission and the Investment Company Act of 1940, the industry didn't really begin to blossom until the mid-1950s. By the end of that decade, there were 155 funds with around $15.8 billion in assets. The sixties saw continued growth, and by 1970, over $48 billion dollars were invested in some 269 funds. Two important changes were about to be introduced into the industry that would propel its growth for the next few decades.

The first of these changes, actually more of an innovation, appeared on the scene in 1976 and was pioneered by John C. Bogle. Many of you may recognize the name, as he is the founder and chief executive officer of the Vanguard Group, the largest no-load mutual fund provider in the country. It was the birth of the Index Mutual Fund, called the First Index Investment Trust, and commonly known today as the Vanguard 500 Index. This was a low-cost alternative to other mutual funds and was designed to track the returns of the major stock indices. By not having to pay fund managers to constantly research stocks and make changes to the portfolios, Mr. Bogle offered investors a cheaper way to participate in the stock market and reap the benefits. There has been much debate over whether or not these low-cost index funds are superior to actively managed mutual funds, and we will discuss that a little more in depth later, and I will give you my personal opinion, but for right now, I just want to give you some background on how these funds came into being.

The other significant change to hit the mutual fund industry happened the following year in 1977 when Peter Lynch took over the management duties of the Fidelity Magellan Fund. Some of you may have already heard of Mr. Lynch, and I'm sure a number of you have some of your assets invested in this fund. Peter Lynch quickly became a superstar in the industry and is widely regarded as the best mutual fund manager of all time. He set a streak of beating the returns of the S&P 500 Index for twelve consecutive years, a record that has recently been tied by Bill Miller of Legg Mason and may be broken by Mr. Miller at the end of 2004, and that is an amazing accomplishment. Peter Lynch not only posted impressive returns for his funds but really thrust into national spotlight the idea of having a superstar fund manager and the assets that name recognition can bring. He certainly paved the way for fund managers' salaries skyrocketing and began the trend of mutual fund companies bidding for the services of these rising stars of the investment world. He no longer manages the funds and hasn't for some time now, but he has written several books, which I recommend that you read because they really are informative, on his investment style and continues to hold somewhat of a legendary status among Wall Street investors.

These two funds incidentally, the Vanguard 500 and the Fidelity Magellan, have been competing for several years now as the two funds with the highest assets under management. Both funds have hit the $100 billion mark at one time, with the Vanguard 500 having the slight edge recently. They both arrived at these points in vastly different ways, one through a low-cost fund marketed directly to investors and the other through the star power of its manager, but they each played a pivotal role in the explosion of mutual funds over the last twenty-five years.

Another driving force behind the popularity of mutual funds over the last quarter of a century was the creation of the Individual Retirement Account (IRA) in 1981. This allowed individuals, even those participating in company-sponsored retirement plans, to contribute $2,000 per year into this account, and depending on certain guidelines, allowed for these contributions to be tax deductible. The money contributed to these accounts needed to be invested and some was invested in stocks and bonds, but people found that the easiest way to invest these sums was to put them in mutual funds. They didn't have to pick or have their stockbroker pick individual stocks, which is a very risky proposition, so they got diversification and could readily access their money if need be because mutual funds had a high degree of liquidity, which meant they could turn around and get a check out to the client in a short period of time. It was a perfect marriage and really proliferated the use of mutual funds in other areas of retirement plans as well, such as the 401(k) and 403(b) plans. This is very likely the arena in which most of us have had exposure to mutual funds, through our retirement plans or IRAs.

That is a brief overview of the fund industry and how it has become such a thriving industry in the United States. We certainly don't need to be experts in the history of mutual funds, but it is important to have some general background on how they came into being and what some of the catalysts for their rapid growth were throughout the years. Now that we have that, we can get into exactly what mutual funds are and how they operate.

Chapter 2 - What is a Mutual Fund?

In short, a mutual fund is a pool of money invested in different financial instruments, such as stocks or bonds, with the goal being to generate either a short or long-term profit. Typically, the funds are gathered from several investors who purchase shares in the mutual fund and then participate either in the gains or losses of the fund. The question most often asked about mutual funds is: Why should I invest in a mutual fund with other people when I could just buy stocks or bonds on my own? There are really two very strong answers to this, and they both make quite a bit of sense:

Diversification—One of the key "buzz" words in the financial industry is diversification. It is a sound principal that I believe all investors should follow. Diversification is simply spreading out the risk associated with investing so that any one particular investment you make doesn't completely destroy your portfolio if it were to under-perform. For example, let's say you decide to invest $5,000 and go online to one of the Internet trading sites such as Ameritrade and buy $5,000 worth of Microsoft stock. It's been an outstandingly performing stock of the last decade, and you think the company is going to do well in the future, too. Again, this is all hypothetical, but right after you make the purchase, news stories began to surface about Microsoft possibly facing some government regulatory charges. The stock price, in turn, begins to slide and your original $5,000 is now worth $3,500. You might start to panic and maybe sell off your shares in Microsoft and look for another stock to invest in. So what have you done? You've bought high and sold low! This is the cardinal mistake. If, however, you had diversified your original $5,000 across different stocks, say $1,000 into five different company stocks, then the momentary drop in Microsoft's stock price wouldn't be so glaring and may, in fact, be offset by the gains in two or three of the other stocks you invested in. Consequently, you could ride out the short-term loss in Microsoft because you believe in the company's long-term potential. This is what a mutual fund provides for you. It can be exceedingly difficult and expensive for the average investor to sufficiently diversify their own portfolio, because it takes a good deal of money, time, and knowledge to do it properly. By pooling your assets with those of other investors, it benefits the entire group by allowing for sound diversification.

Knowledge—Quite frankly, common investors like you and I just don't have the time to thoroughly research every company we're going to invest in. It takes a lot of work, and even then, it demands a certain proficiency in interpreting all the data once we have gathered it. It really is a full-time job. The money manager, the person or persons in charge of investing the assets of the mutual fund, is compensated, and in some cases overly compensated, to compile and analyze all this information and make the final decision on where to invest the assets of the fund. In other words, it's letting the professionals of the financial world invest our money for us. In most walks of life, when you look to contract someone out to either work on your house or you look for a mechanic to find out what that thumping noise is under your hood, you want the best you can find. The same concept applies here. Find the best person who specializes in that field and let him or her do their job.

If you have the money, time, desire, and most importantly, knowledge and want to invest in individual stocks, then by all means, go for it. But I'll give you this disclaimer: The chances of you being a successful stock-picker over a long period of time, at least ten years, are very slim. I'm not saying that it can't be done, but I've talked with and personally seen a great number of people lose large sums of money when they thought they could "beat the street," meaning they could do better then the money managers on Wall Street. The vast majority of those who failed had one thing in common, they had supreme confidence in their abilities, and rightly so, because many of them were some of the brightest people I've ever met, but they just didn't have the knowledge about the financial world that they thought they had.

Chapter 3 - Types of Mutual Funds

The discussion we could have on the different types of mutual funds offered today could be a virtually never-ending one. There are so many types and classes of funds that just looking at a company's lineup of funds can be intimidating. I really just want to cover two of the most dominating styles of investing and then a few of the most popular classes of funds. I'll then give you an example of a "style box" that will give you a visual reference for what we're about to discuss.

The predominant styles of investing today are growth and value. The following question will often be asked of a money manager: Are you a growth or value-based manager? So what in the world does that mean?

Growth investing is a style where the money manager is seeking out investments that have a large potential for growth over the next few years or the next decade, depending on the time horizon of the fund's investors. Well, this seems pretty obvious that of course we want companies that are going to grow rapidly and avoid the ones that are going to go bankrupt! And you're right, in fact, both styles of investing, growth and value, are looking for companies that are going to grow in the future, but the second part of this equation is where the two styles differ in philosophy and that is on the price of the investment. Growth managers are willing to pay more, and in some cases, over-pay for the future performance of a stock because they believe that the future potential outweighs the current cost. If it takes paying more than what the stock is worth today in order to add it to the portfolio and reap the benefits in the future, then so be it. So a growth-oriented money manager is looking for those explosive growth companies that can become the dominant force in their industry in the next few years, such as a Microsoft or an Intel when they were just getting off the ground.

The value investor, on the other hand, is more concerned about the price of the investment. The most renowned value investor of all time and one of the richest men in the country, Warren Buffet, really helped pioneer this investment style. Mr. Buffet and other value managers believe that a company's value can be determined by analyzing its financial statements, market share, quality of management, etc. This value is usually referred to as the intrinsic value of a company. If the current stock price of this company is substantially lower than the intrinsic value, then it would be a good value buy. The theory holds that the market, at this time, for whatever reason, is undervaluing this company, and eventually, the market will come to its senses, value the stock as it should, and we would have made money. For example, let's say Coca-Cola stock, one of Mr. Buffet's favorites, had an intrinsic value of $60 a share. The market price at the time was $45 a share. That's a perfect value buy. It's a large multi-national company that is the dominant force in its industry, and basically, the stock is on sale! Let's grab it at $45, and eventually, it could take several years, but the market will correct itself and will value Coca-Cola stock at $60 a share, and we would have made a 33% gain.

That is a nuts-and-bolts explanation of the difference in the styles, and I hope it made sense and clarified in your minds the basic differences in the two philosophies. So which one is better? The answer to that is neither. They are both fundamentally sound, and again, if history is any indicator, both styles fall in and out of favor. Usually, one style is the "hot" style for a few years, and then it shifts back to the other style. Recently, since the dot.com bubble burst in 2000, value investing was in favor up through 2003 when the stock market rebounded, and then, in that year, it seemed that growth became the more preferred style. The truth is that both are effective and an investor should have funds with both styles in his or her portfolio.

There is a third style, which really isn't its own style, it's a blend of both growth and value. Not surprisingly, it's called a blended style! I want you to be aware of it because you will hear the term, but in essence, it is a fund that tries to use a happy medium between the two styles. The fund will have both growth plays and value plays, trying to hedge their bets. I personally think this is a good strategy as well. It allows the fund some flexibility to take advantage of the swings in preference between growth and value.

Mutual funds are also broken out by what sector of the market they specialize in. The three most common of these specializations are referred to as large-cap, mid-cap, and small-cap. The "cap" stands for capitalization and gives the investor an idea of what kind of companies the fund primarily invests in. This capitalization refers to the market capitalization of a company. Basically, it means what the company is worth, after taking into account all of their assets. Each fund company varies slightly on the parameters for categorizing a company into one of these sectors, but, generally speaking, the following guidelines apply:

Small-Cap Stock—less than $2 billion in market capitalization
Mid-Cap Stock—between $2 billion and $10 billion in market capitalization
Large-Cap Stock—greater than $10 billion in market capitalization

For example, when you hear an investment representative say, "This is a large-cap value fund," it means that the vast majority of the holdings of that fund are going to be stocks of companies with a market cap of more than $10 billion and are currently undervalued in the market. The opposite of this example would be a small-cap growth fund which would be investing in the stocks of fledgling companies with a market cap of under $2 billion, but which have the potential for explosive growth and may become the next Microsoft or IBM. Here is the example of the "style box" that I mentioned earlier. Mutual funds will generally be pegged into one of these boxes, and that is done to give you, the investor, some sense of the underlying philosophy of the investment you are purchasing:

Value	Blend	Growth
Large–Cap	Large–Cap	Large–Cap
Mid–Cap	Mid–Cap	Mid–Cap
Small–Cap	Small–Cap	Small-Cap

Each investor must decide where and how much to invest in any of these styles, and that determination is going to correlate directly with how much risk he or she is comfortable taking. Generally speaking, growth-driven funds have more risk associated with them than value funds. Also along those lines, small-cap stock funds have the most risk associated with them, followed by mid-cap funds, and then large-cap funds. So on one end of the spectrum, a small-cap growth fund would probably have the highest risk associated with it while a large-cap value fund would likely have the least risk. Again, these are just generalities, but they give you an idea of where you might fall in the above style box. If you're the type of investor who wants to try and hit a homerun and have the best performance possible with little regard if you have down periods along the way where you are losing money, then you have a high risk tolerance. On the flip side, if not losing money at any cost is your number one primary goal, then you would fall in the risk averse category. The majority of investors usually fall somewhere in the middle of these two extremes. We want good returns on our investments, but we want to accomplish it by taking as little risk as possible. Mutual fund risk is generally measured using a calculation referred to as beta. A fund's beta measures its risk relative to a given index, such as the S&P 500. The beta ranges on a scale between 0 and 2, and without getting into specific details of how beta is calculated, just know that the lower the beta number is the less risk that is generally associated with that fund. Conversely, a beta number well over 1, say 1.2 for example, would generally indicate a riskier fund. It's not necessary that everyone be experts in all the intricacies of how beta is calculated and how it works, I just want you to be aware of the term, and that generally speaking, the higher the beta the riskier the investment.

I know we have already used the S&P 500 Index extensively in our discussions so far, and for good reason, as it is the most widely used benchmark of how the stock market is performing, but it is certainly not the only investment you should consider. We know that the S&P 500 is made up of 500 large-cap stocks, but history bears out that the most effective strategy for consistently outperforming the S&P 500 Index is to diversify your investments across all three market capitalizations. The stock market tends to be very cyclical in that different classes of stocks tend to outperform the other classes in any given year. These stock classes are said to be "in favor" in that given year. For example, one year, small-cap stocks might be head and shoulders above mid and large-cap stocks in terms of performance, and the next year, large-cap stocks may be "in favor" and have the best performance figures. Since no one can consistently and accurately predict which particular stock class will be "in favor" in any given year, the most sound strategy is to diversify your investments across all three classes.

Figures show that investing in indices that track all three stock classes, so one-third of your investment in small, mid, and large-cap stocks, outperformed the S&P 500 over the last ten years. From 1994 to 2003, the S&P 500 had an annualized return of 11.06%; whereas using the one-third strategy, it had an annualized return of 12.30%. (The other indices used to obtain these figures were the S&P 400 and the S&P 600, which track mid-cap and small-cap stocks respectively.) This diversification idea outperformed the S&P 500 by 1.24% per year, and more importantly, it did so without incurring any additional risk. The risk of the investments, as calculated by their standard deviations, was identical. My point here is that although the S&P 500 will be mentioned extensively in this book and in the media, don't feel that you must confine yourself to only investing in large-cap stocks because you will be sacrificing performance by putting all your eggs in one basket.

One final thing I want to touch on in this section is the emergence of sector-specific funds. Sector specific, in this case, is not really referring to the above style box but rather to a specific sector of the economy that a fund invests in. I want to make the distinction because you will hear the term "sector fund," and this is more than likely what is being referenced. These funds gained great popularity in the late 1990s due to the rising market and the skyrocketing growth of technology and healthcare stocks. Since these stocks, in particular, were showing remarkable returns year after year, fund companies launched funds specifically devoted to investing in these stocks. These devoted funds invested solely in the technology sector of healthcare sector stocks. Hence, the name "sector funds" was born. There are a multitude of funds today covering various sectors of the marketplace, from technology to healthcare, to financial services, to precious metals. They can show remarkable short-term returns, especially if their particular sector is in favor with the market at the time. However, due to their lack of diversification, which we discussed earlier, they tend to have more risk associated with them. Sector funds such as these can be a valuable part, all be it a small part, of an investor's portfolio, but for common investors such as ourselves investing for the long term, we should probably at most hold 10% of our assets in investments such as these.

Chapter 4 - Mutual Funds and What They Cost

Like any other business or service, mutual funds have costs associated with them. These costs can range from initial purchase costs to ongoing expenses in running the funds to surrender charges for selling your shares. We will discuss all of these funds as they vary depending on what types of share class you own, but before we get into the discussion, I want to impress upon you how important a fund's expenses are. They should be the most important factor you consider when choosing a fund to invest in. After we discuss all of the different types of fees associated with them, I'll provide you with some data that will crystallize why I feel so strongly about this. I relate it to the axiom used when purchasing real estate: What's the most important thing when considering a real estate purchase? Location, location, location. The same applies for our discussion. What's the most important aspect to consider when investing in a mutual fund? Fees, fees, fees!

I'm taking the obvious for granted here, in that performance is going to be the first measuring stick used when narrowing our choices of investments. I doubt anyone of us would look at a lineup of investments and find the one with the worst performance numbers and say. "That's the one I want to invest in!" Of course, the first criterion is going to be the returns of the mutual funds, but that just goes without saying. Making an informed decision about which well-performing fund to invest in lies within examining how high the expenses of those individual funds are. This will become clear at the end of this chapter, but for now, let's start our discussion of what types of charges and expenses we might incur when investing in a given fund.

Sales Charges

The first charge we may encounter is referred to as a sales charge or sales load. This is charged to us when we first purchase shares in a given fund. The sales charge is generally used to pay the broker from whom you purchased the fund his or her commission. The reason I say that we may encounter an upfront charge such as this one depends on what class of share we buy. Mutual funds typically offer three types of share classes to individual investors: class A, B, and C shares as they are commonly referred to. You may hear other class share names such as Y or L shares, but typically, for the common investor such as you and I, it is A, B, and C shares. The difference between them has to due with their fee structure. With regards to upfront sales charges, they breakdown the following way:

Class A shares—These shares charge an upfront sales charge to the investor, the amount of which varies on the size of the investment, the larger the investment, the lower the charge. For example, if we invested $1,000 into a typical class A share fund, the upfront charge might be 4.5%, meaning that $45 out of our original $1,000 would be deducted immediately and used to pay the commission to our broker. Rather then investing a full $1,000, our initial investment would only be $955.

Class B shares—Class B shares don't charge an upfront sales charge, so if we used the same $1,000 to buy a B share of a fund, our full $1,000 would get invested for us. The mutual fund company pays the commission to the broker so we don't get charged. Why wouldn't everybody buy these shares? This sounds too good to be true. Well, you're right, it is. The mutual fund company makes up for this by charging higher ongoing expenses to the investor and adds on another charge, called a contingent deferred sales charge (CDSC). This is a different type of charge that we are going to cover in the next section, but basically, it is a percentage charged to you for selling your shares within the first few years after your investment. For example, if you sold your shares after two years of being in the fund, then you would be charged perhaps 5% in order to recoup the original commission the company paid out to the broker. After this CDSC period is over, typically after eight years, these shares convert to class A shares and the higher ongoing asset-based charges also reduce accordingly. We will go more in depth into these charges in just a bit.

Class C shares—These shares typically have no upfront charge either, although certain companies may charge an upfront sales load of 1% in exchange for lower ongoing asset-based charges. These asset-based charges are usually on par with the class B share expenses; however, they don't convert to A shares at any point. Consequently, the fees don't get reduced in the future. The reason you, as an investor, might be interested in this particular share class over the B share is the liquidity factor. By liquidity, I'm referring to how quickly you can access your money without having to pay a CDSC. Typically, class C shares have a CDSC of 1% for a period of one year, meaning that after that first year, you could pull all your money out of the fund and pay no penalty. These shares are the favorite class of shares to sell by a large number of investment representatives due to their commission structure. Let me run through an example of the commission structure of each of these share classes because it's very important that you have an idea of how your investment representative is getting paid on a trade and it could shed some light on why he or she seems to be leading you in a certain direction.

We already touched on how investment representatives get paid on the sale of A shares. A certain percent of the money you invest, we assumed 4.5%, is set aside to pay the representative their commission. This is pretty straightforward; you purchase the fund and the broker gets paid that percent after the sale and that is it. With B and C shares, the investment representative also gets paid an upfront commission, as well as what is called a trail commission. A trail commission is a payment made to the representative in the future, usually after thirteen months, based on the value of the assets within the fund. The amount of this trail commission is referred to in the financial industry in terms of basis points. A basis point is one one-hundredth of a percent. For example, one basis point would be equal to .01 percent. Most B shares, along with paying a percent of the investment representative's commission upfront, start paying a twenty-five basis point (.25%) trail commission to the investment representative, usually beginning in the fifteenth month following the sale. So every year, the representative who sold you the fund will get paid .25% based on whatever the value of the fund is. If the fund performs fairly well, then the amount of the trail commission check they receive goes up every year. I hope it now makes sense to you why trail commissions are so important to investment representatives. They are getting paid residual commissions on a sale they already made! It doesn't get much easier than that. They walk into their office in January to start the year, and they know that those commission checks will be coming to them regardless of whether they make any new sales during that year or not. This leads into why C shares have grown so rapidly in popularity with investment representatives. The general payout structure for the representatives when they sell a C share is they receive 1% (100 basis points) upfront, and in the thirteenth month, they begin receiving a trail of another 100 basis points. So, in exchange for giving up those percentage points upfront that they would have received by selling a B-share, they now receive four times as big of a commission check. This is what is widely referred to as "annuitizing" their business. That means they have streams of income in the form of trail commissions they can count on every year from sales they already made, which reduces their need to generate new sales every year. Since we expect the funds that we invest in to grow over time, so does the amount of the trail check paid to the investment representative, because remember that the 100-basis point trail is paid based off the value of the account. The investment representatives certainly know this and generally have been trying to increase the amount of large trail commission paying products they sell.

Let me just give you some quick numbers to maybe help crystallize how powerful this information is. If an investment representative has $25 million of assets under his or her management that are all in C-share mutual funds, that is $250,000 in trail checks they will receive that year! I mean, think about it, that is $250,000 they can count on at the start of the year in January even if they don't make one sale the entire year. Not a bad way to start every year, right? That is the reason why you'll get presented with C shares of a particular fund to buy. It is so important that you be aware of this.

Which share class is the best: A, B, or C? In the vast majority of cases, the common investor, such as you and I, when presented with all three classes, should always buy A shares. If your goals are long term, with time horizons of at least five years and especially ten years and beyond, then you should always buy A shares. The savings you will gain with the lower expenses you pay every year will far outweigh the percent of upfront fees you have to pay. You are 100% liquid from the start with A shares, so you can take withdrawals if need be or move your money to another mutual fund if you desire, and if you plan on making additional investments, you are eligible to receive breakpoints on your future purchases. Mutual funds have a sliding scale of how much you pay in upfront sales charges based on the amount of the purchase you're going to make. For example,

Purchase amount	Sales Charge
$0-$49,999	4.5%
$50,000-$99,999	3.5%
$100,000-$249,999	2.5%

If we bought the fund for an original investment of $25,000, based on this scale, we would have paid 4.5% in an upfront charge. Let's assume that the following year, we want to invest an additional $25,000. Normally, we would pay the 4.5% on our $25,000 addition, but with breakpoints, the mutual fund company will look at the amount of assets you already have invested with them and add those assets to your additional payment when calculating the sales charge. We already invested our original $25,000 so that will get added to our addition of $25,000 giving us a total of $50,000 invested in the fund. Consequently, we will only pay 3.5% as a sales charge on the $25,000 addition. Can anyone see why this would be disadvantageous to investment representatives? That's right, the amount of their commission check is getting reduced based on these breakpoints. Rather then getting paid an additional 4.5% on the $25,000 addition, they are only getting paid 3.5% and not receiving any trail commissions. This wouldn't be the case if they sold either of the other two share classes. Incidentally, breakpoints with most mutual fund companies apply to direct family members, meaning parents, grandparents, siblings, children, and grandchildren. So if your parents have a significant amount of their assets invested with a mutual fund company, you will be able to combine your purchase amount with their assets to calculate your sales charge breakpoint.

I never like to say never, because I don't believe there are many absolutes in this world, but if your goals for investing are to pay for your retirement, put your children through school, buy a vacation home, or anything that would be a long-term goal of ten years or more, then you should be purchasing A shares if you are going to invest in mutual funds. B shares do have the advantage of investing your entire purchase amount immediately, but the higher fees that you will incur over those first eight years will cost you far more. I know it's tough to conceptualize because you can't see the fees that you will be paying in the future, but keep in mind that those fees are based on the value of your account each year. If the fund is performing well, which we hope it will, the dollar amount of those extra fees is increasing every year! After those first eight years, the total dollar amount you will have paid in extra fees will exceed and in some cases, far exceed what you would have initially paid in upfront charges if you had bought A shares.

Contingent Deferred Sales Charge (CDSC)

We've mentioned these charges already in our discussion of B and C share classes of mutual funds, but I just want to give you a little more information on them. We covered the upfront sales charge already, and you will often hear the CDSC referred to as a "back-end" charge because it is charged to you when you sell all your shares of a particular fund or take a sizeable withdrawal from that fund. Assuming we invested $1,000 into B shares of a particular mutual fund, and we wanted to sell our shares of that fund after three years, we would incur one of these "back-end" charges. This charge would be based on a surrender charge schedule provided to you at the time you purchased the fund which outlines what percent the CDSC is in each particular year. One of these schedules may look like this:

Year	CDSC%
1	6%
2	5%
3	4%
4	4%
5	3%
6	3%
7	2%
8	1%

Based on this schedule, if you decide to liquidate all your holdings in that fund in year three, you would pay a 4% charge. If we assume our $1,000 grew to $1,500, then we would pay a charge of $1,500 x .04 = $60. This is the mutual fund company's way of recouping the broker commission that they paid out during the initial purchase, since all of your $1,000 got invested immediately. Another thing to keep in mind with products that have a CDSC is that the vast majority of them start a new CDSC schedule on every addition you make. Continuing our example of the $1,000 initial investment, say you make a $1,000 addition two years later, that $1,000 addition will start its own surrender schedule! In this case, all of your money will not be surrendered charge free after eight years, only the initial amount will. It's an important aspect to be aware of because many times, it's not properly explained when you make the initial purchase.

It would seem that if your investment goal is long term and you have absolutely no intention of touching the money, then the CDSC isn't something you need to be concerned with. By the time you need to tap into the account, the CDSC will be over. However, remember the golden rule of selecting a mutual fund: fees, fees, fees! You will be paying those higher ongoing fees for those eight years after your initial purchase, and they will cost you performance returns in the long run. That is why for so many of you reading this book, you should without question be purchasing A shares. If you're not, you should sit down and review your investment goals and objectives. If short-term liquidity is important to you, meaning you may very likely need access to your investment dollars within a few years, then holding some C shares is probably suitable for you because if there is a CDSC associated with them, it most likely is only for the first year. If your goal is long term, as we discussed earlier, then A shares are your best choice. When you sit down and look at your portfolio and find that you do hold B-shares, you need to ask yourself why? I'm hard pressed to think of an example when you would ever want to own B shares! The expenses are typically in line with those of C shares, so if liquidity is of priority to you, there is no reason to buy them over C shares and pay the same expenses but also incur a seven or eight-year CDSC. If long-term investing is your goal, then we have already stated that A shares are the superior choice due to their lower operating expenses. This is the reason that you see very few B shares being sold. So please, if you are looking to invest in any mutual fund, don't even consider purchasing their B shares.

Annual Fund Operating Expenses

These are the annual expenses associated with the operation and distribution of mutual funds that I have been referring to as the ongoing expenses paid by the shareholders every year. They include the management fees, the distribution and marketing fees, and other expenses associated with running the mutual fund. These are the expenses that differ with each share class. A shares have the lowest expenses while B and C shares have higher expenses. A mutual fund's total expenses are expressed as an expense ratio. The expense ratio measures the fund's total annual expenses as a percent of the fund's net assets. A quick example would be if a fund's total expense ratio were 1%, then this would represent a 1% charge to the fund's net assets every year. So you, as an investor, would pay 1% of the assets you have invested with the fund every year. The total expense ratio of any mutual fund for any of its share classes can be found in the fee table in the front of the fund's prospectus. A prospectus is a legal document that every mutual fund must file with the SEC. A copy must be given to the investor at the time of purchase. It is an extremely wordy and boring book to read, I can testify to that from experience! However, it is also a wealth of information and the fee table is a section you should pay particular attention to, and if there is anything you see in there that doesn't make sense to you or you don't understand, then ask your investment representative. If he or she can't explain it to you, then get a representative from the mutual fund company themselves on the phone to give a clear explanation, and if after that, you're still not satisfied then delay the purchase! Consult with another investment representative or feel free to contact me, and I'll assist you! Just don't finalize any sale if there is anything you're unclear of or that you don't understand, because remember, these are your investment dollars and how to invest them is one of the most important decisions you will ever make.

The management fees involved in the annual operating expenses go to pay the investment company that actually manages and invests the fund's assets. It includes paying the portfolio manager, the research analysts, and other personnel that are responsible for the performance of the fund. Arguments have been made on both sides of the fence about how important good money managers are. The supporters of top-flight money management argue that only the best and brightest of the financial world can deliver consistent positive returns that beat the S&P 500 and other indices. The detractors, on the other hand, argue that the overwhelming majority of fund managers have failed to significantly outperform the Index, so investors are better off by just buying Index mutual funds and saving themselves the extra expenses associated with hiring money managers. I personally see the benefits of both. The primary benefit of a top-level portfolio manager is really highlighted in a down market, such as the one we've had the last few years. Having a person or, in most cases, a team of individuals analyzing the market and the health of certain companies can be quite beneficial because it can limit the losses a fund may incur during a down market, often called a bear market. When the market is going up and up, such as it was during the mid to late 1990s, then every fund's performance looks fantastic! It makes it more difficult to distinguish the importance of a gifted portfolio manager from just an indexed mutual fund. During those up markets, called bull markets, the index funds are showing excellent returns, and it seems like a no-brainer to invest in them and save on the management expenses because even if the managed funds are beating the index by a few points, it doesn't seem enough to justify paying the extra fees, and most investors are content with the stellar returns they are seeing from their index funds. However, in the bear markets, as I said before, is where the cream will rise to the top and the few true quality fund managers will separate themselves. These managed funds should perform more favorably in these down markets because there is someone steering the ship and adjusting to the changing market conditions. Index funds, on the other hand, are on autopilot. They simply are buying the stocks in the S&P 500 Index without regard to how the particular industry or sector of the market that a stock is in is doing and whether or not that stock is positioned to perform well in the foreseeable future. In order to really get a good grasp of whether or not a fund manager is of top quality, look to see how that manager has performed in a down market. That is the real test. It reminds me of the old adage: "All boats float in a rising tide, but when the tide goes out, you can tell who's been swimming naked!"

Mutual funds are compared to one another based on their style and the cap sectors that we discussed earlier, and this comparison is referred to as a fund's Lipper average. Lipper is a company that tracks the returns of funds and compares them to their peer group, funds with the same general investment guidelines based on style and cap holdings, and then ranks each fund. They rank the funds based on quartile rankings, so obviously, every fund wants to be ranked in the top quartile and also arrive at the average return for all of those particular funds. So when asking about the fund's performance, we are first going to ask to see how the fund performed in a down market, right? Then the follow-up questions have to be: How did this fund compare to its Lipper peer group during that time? Did it beat its Lipper average? What quartile did it rank in?

This will instantly do two things. One, it will show your level of investment knowledge and gain you instant credibility with the investment representative. It shows that you will not be talked into any kind of sale without first thoroughly understanding what kind of fund you are purchasing and whether or not that fund is deserving of your investment dollars. The second and most important thing it does is provide you with the crucial information you need to make the proper investment decision. Is this mutual fund and this fund manager going to protect me in the those down markets and provide me the solid returns I expect in the bull markets? As I have previously stated, history is no guarantee of the future, but if you can answer yes to these questions based on how a particular fund has performed in the past in both bull and bear markets, then it is a fund that is likely worthy of your investment.

The second major expense that comprises the annual operating expense of a mutual fund is the distribution fees. These fees cover the expense of marketing the fund and selling the shares, paying for advertising, printing, and mailing the prospectuses to investors, and the printing and mailing of any other sales literature. In the prospectus, these fees are referred to as 12b-1 fees. The name 12b-1 just comes from the SEC ruling that authorizes mutual funds to charge these fees. Absolutely, ask about these fees before you ever buy a mutual fund. Ask the questions: Does this fund charge a 12b-1 fee? Your investment representative will know, or at least should know, what that means. You need to ask the questions because these fees can be sort of hidden when you make the initial purchase, unless you ask these questions or look at the fee table in the prospectus.

The SEC doesn't limit the size of 12b-1 fees that funds may charge, however the NASD has ruled that 12b-1 fees used for marketing and distribution expenses cannot exceed .75%, or 75 basis points, of a fund's average net assets per year. So, .75 is the maximum that could be charged to you by a mutual fund as a 12b-1 fee. Now, this may not sound like much, but at the end of this section, we are going to run through an example that will clearly illustrate how just a few basis points of difference in fees can make a tremendous difference in the long-term returns you see.

The final component of a mutual fund's annual expenses is categorized as "other expenses." As you can gather from the name, this category basically includes all the miscellaneous expenses associated with running a mutual fund that don't fall into one of the previously mentioned categories. These would include custodial expenses, legal and accounting expenses, transfer agent costs, and other administrative expenses. This would also include customer service agents that investors could call to ask questions about a particular fund within a company.

Chapter 5 - How Does This Affect Me?

It's great that we have all this information and knowledge now, but I'm fairly positive that this is the question that is going through all your minds right now:

How does this really affect me and why should I care?

I mean, we are talking about the difference of only tenths of a percent between some funds. If the funds you invested in are showing solid and consistent performance returns, does the .2% or .3% difference in fees really matter? Absolutely, it matters! Remember, the first rule of investing in mutual funds: Fees, fees, fees! Let's run through an example to illustrate this point.

Our assumption here is going to be a thirty-year time horizon and for simplicity's sake, we assume we invested $100,000 to start. I know most common investors, such as ourselves, don't have $100,000 to invest, but even if it's only $1,000, we can shave two numbers off the end of these figures and come up with a pretty accurate portrait. The $100,000 amount is just a good, round starting number. If we also assume a gross annual return of 10%, then at the end of our thirty-year time frame, we would have $1,745,000, a very impressive number! I think all of us would be happy with that sort of return. Now, notice that this is a GROSS return number, so we haven't factored expenses into the equation yet. So, let's take a look at these same numbers and take into account some average fund fees.

The first fee assumption we make is that we invested all of our funds into index funds. Remember that index funds generally have lower expenses because they don't have to pay a star money manager to run the fund. The average index fund expense is around .2%. That translates into about $92,000 in expenses over that thirty-year period leaving us with a net amount of $1,653,000. This is certainly a reasonable price to pay for that kind of return on your investment, but remember, this is assuming the funds were invested in an averagely expensed index mutual fund.

The second assumption will assume we invest in large-cap mutual funds, which have an average cost of roughly .8%. It doesn't sound like a big jump in fees because you are still paying under 1% for professional money management, but let's take a look at the total dollar impact on our investment. Fees of .8% translate into a dollar amount of $343,000. That is a significant difference, leaving us with a final dollar amount of $1,402,000, or $251,000 less than the index fund investment. I hope you're starting to see the impact of these fund expenses.

In our third scenario, we assume that the $100,000 was invested in a well-diversified (remember that buzz word) portfolio of funds. Well, the simple average of expenses across all mutual funds is 1.08%. That increases our total cost in a dollar figure to $447,000. That is roughly one quarter of our entire return! The original $100,000 grew to $1,745,000 so we saw a gain of $1,645,000. Well, if we paid $447,000 in fees, that is over 25% of our gain that we lost in expenses! But when you look at the fees in terms of a percent, such as 1.08%, it doesn't convey that same message. So our total dollar return for this scenario comes out to $1,298,000.

Remember earlier when I mentioned the Legg Mason Value Fund, which is run by a gentleman named Bill Miller, and I stated that he and his fund were about to break Peter Lynch's record of beating the S&P 500 Index for a an incredible thirteen straight years. It looks like a slam-dunk to invest money in this fund since it outperforms the primary benchmark for the market every year. However, when we take a closer look at the fund, the expenses don't seem to justify the returns. The expense of the Legg Mason Value Fund is 1.72%, much higher then the fees we have discussed thus far. But in all fairness, doesn't the fund deserve to charge higher fees based on their track record? Maybe that's true, but not to this extent, and let me show you why. In our same scenario as before, the 1.72% expense ratio on this fund translates into $657,000 in fees. That is an astounding number! Almost 40% of our gains over that thirty-year time span would go to paying expenses. But again, when these funds are being sold, the expense ratios get expressed in a percent, which is much easier for the consumer (i.e., us) to swallow because it's not a tangible number that we associate with a dollar amount. Obviously, the argument for the Legg Mason fund is that you are paying the higher fees for outperforming the indices themselves and the funds that track them. All right, let's take a look at that argument. The Legg Mason fund has beaten the S&P 500 by an average of 2.68% annually over its remarkable run. Those are solid numbers, but remember that the average index expense is .2% whereas the fees on the Legg Mason fund are 1.72%. So the investor is paying 1.52% higher in fees every year for that performance. A little simple math show us that, in effect, the Legg Mason fund is only outperforming the S&P 500 by 1.14% annually (2.68% to 1.52%). Let's not forget that since the expenses are a percent of the assets, as the investment in the funds grows, this disparity in fees becomes larger and larger every year when expressed as a total dollar figure.

People are going to say that I'm bashing the Legg Mason Value Fund and Bill Miller. I'm not bashing them at all; I'm simply trying to explain to common investors such as myself how great an impact fees can have on our investments. I certainly wouldn't invest solely in the Legg Mason fund, because there are much better buys in the market, but I would consider it as a part of a portfolio, probably a small part, but performance figures like that can't just be ignored. Personally, a few of the funds that I like and hold investments in are the Hartford Capital Appreciation Fund and a favorite large-cap fund of mine is the Clipper Fund. The Clipper Fund has an expense ratio of about 1.07% and has actually outperformed the Legg Mason Value Fund over the last fifteen years by 14.8% to 14.3%. I've made the analogy already, and I'll make it again here: You always want the odds on your side. Mutual fund companies, and more so insurance companies which we'll talk about in the variable annuity section, are like casinos. They play the odds and collect fees based on those odds. Finding low expenses and still getting solid performance returns is the most effective tool we have in evening up those odds.

Below here is a table of my personal opinion of what the maximum range of fees we as investors should pay for certain types of mutual funds. This is just a general guideline and is by no means written in stone. Generally speaking, the best performing funds in these categories will have expense ratios below the average because higher fees are usually a drag on performance, but that is not always the case. I didn't include index funds on this list because, generally speaking, their fund expenses don't vary all that much and stay relatively consistent around .2%. So you can use that number as a benchmark for the index funds, but it's been my experience that you won't see much deviation from that number, and if you do, you need to ask why. So here are some of my fee recommendations for you to keep in mind when deciding to invest in a particular mutual fund:

Fund Type	Average Expense	Max you should pay
Large-Cap	1.25%	1–1.10%
Mid-Cap	1.59%	1.10–1.20%
Small-Cap	1.58%	1.10–1.20%
Sector	1.51%	1.05–1.15%
International	1.72%	1.20–1.30%
High-yield Bond	1.40%	.90–1.00%
Corporate Bond	1.10%	.80–.90%

There is one final thing I want to talk about in this section of fees. That is the theory that as funds accumulate assets, their overall expense ratios drop due to the fact that expenses are being spread out over more assets and more shareholders. This was an idea I first learned about in college, and then it was later reinforced when I entered the job world, working for a mutual fund and variable annuity distribution firm. It made sense to me, and I never really questioned it and assumed it to be true. However, in doing my research for this book, I found the opposite to be true. As of the end of June of 2004, the average fund expense ratio was 1.52%, an increase of .13% from the end of 1987! With the massive inflow of investor dollars to mutual funds over that time frame, you would certainly have expected fund expenses to decrease, but that just hasn't been the case. I also found some interesting quotes from a few money managers and executive officers at a few money management companies that I wanted to share with you. The first few quotes are from Bridget Macaskill, president and chief executive officer of Oppenheimer funds. Oppenheimer's fund expenses have risen about .11% over the last decade, and she attributes this rise to providing investors with more information, education, and Internet and telephone access.

She said, "Really, they (investors) haven't paid for that."

Is that right? So I guess they provided all of those services out of the kindness of their hearts. We've just seen what the impact of a .11% increase in fees can have on a portfolio and the total dollars in fees it can translate into for a money management company, so my response to Ms. Macaskill would be that we, the investors, have in fact paid for it. Another quote I saw from Ms. Macaskill was:

"What really matters to the investor is the return on investment after expenses. If returns are lower, then fees will matter more."

In a sense, she is correct in some aspects of this statement. Investors such as you and I haven't really cared about expenses in up markets because we were only given that number as a percent, and not a dollar amount. However, after seeing the impact that fees can have as a dollar amount on our investments, I think most of us would disagree with her.

Another great quote on this subject came from David Brady, a fund manager for Stein Roe. This one is really great:

"With a market that is up 30%, 125-150 basis points don't really mean much. But in a flat or down market it's going to make a big difference."

I really have no idea why Mr. Brady would make a statement like this unless he just hasn't done any research whatsoever on the impact of fund fees. He's right that investors haven't cared about expenses in up markets in the past, but that is because they didn't know the full impact of the fees, not because they weren't important! Fees in up markets should be MORE important to investors like us because that is when the lower expense funds will provide us with a greater total dollar return. I mean, we just laid out the difference that fees can have and what an impact just 40 or 50 basis points can have over time, not to mention 125-150 basis points! It's obvious to me that Mr. Brady either has absolutely no concept of the effect of these fees, or more likely, he has a very good grasp on them and that is why he justifies them.

Mickey Roth, president and chief executive officer of USAA Investment Management Company, said, "Do funds compete on cost? Generally, the answer to that is 'No.'"

I hate to break it to Mr. Roth but the cost of a fund relative to the fund's performance is exactly what we as common investors should be buying on. Fund companies and executives such as Mr. Roth don't want their companies competing based on cost because it's been there own little secret for some time now about how much money these annual fees generate. They don't want the general public knowing the impact full fees can have on the returns of an investment because it would mean they would have to actually reduce their fees, heaven forbid, and maybe even take pay cuts. By expressing the fund fees in terms of a percentage, it allows the company's fund to be packaged in such a way that the impact of the fees gets lost on the customer. That is exactly what they want. That is exactly how these funds have been sold for the last few decades, and it's time we, as investors, starting calling these companies to the carpet on the fees they have been charging us.

There is a helpful tool that you can use on the SEC Website which will show the impact that fees can have on a given fund. It's called the Mutual Fund Cost Calculator, and it's a great tool. I would highly recommend that everyone take advantage of it before making an investment decision on a particular fund. It will compute the costs of different mutual funds for you and show just how those costs can add up over time and eat into your returns.

Chapter 6 - Taxes: How they Impact our Decision

Taxes are, of course, a major concern for investors at all times. How can they be reduced, deferred, or maybe even eliminated? My goal for this section is not to engage in a detailed tax discussion for two reasons: One, I'm not a tax expert and will never claim to be. There are plenty of CPAs, tax attorneys, and tax-related software at our disposal that we don't need to be experts in the tax code. The second reason is that it's boring! I don't know about anyone else but I know I don't wait on edge for the day that the tax code gets published every year and immediately buy a copy of *Tax Facts* and settle in for an exciting night. If we delved into any lengthy conversation about taxes, not only would you fall asleep trying to read this book, but I would fall asleep just trying to write it! However, it is important that we have a basic understanding of how mutual funds are taxed and what causes investors such as ourselves to pay those taxes in any given year.

There are two basic categories that investments fall into with regards to taxes, and they are dividends and capital gains. Capital gains taxes are in fact broken down even further into short-term gains and long-term gains. Each is treated differently for tax purposes. This may sound like it's getting complicated already, but once we discuss it, you'll see that it's relatively straightforward.

First, let's just talk about dividends. Dividends are payments that companies make to the owners of their stocks. In essence, it's a return of the earnings the company has generated in a given year. The company pays them out to their shareholders on a per share basis. For example, a company might pay a dividend of $0.10 per share. So for every share that an investor owned, they would be paid $0.10. An investor who owned one share, in turn, would be responsible for paying taxes on that $0.10 payment they received. Dividend payments such as these are taxable at the investor's current tax bracket. There is no other calculation necessary. That $0.10 you or I received from owning that stock would just be included in your taxable income for the year, and if you were in the 28% tax bracket that is what would be applied to the dividend payment. I told you it was painless and straightforward.

This same concept applies to mutual funds as well. Remember the fund itself owns the shares of stock. So the dividends get paid to the fund and the fund, in turn, funnels those payments to the investors of the fund (i.e., you and me). These distributions from the fund to us as dividends are treated the same way as if we had owned the stock or bond personally. The fund will have a declared ex-dividend date, which is the date that any shareholder who invested into the fund before this date will share in the dividend distributions and be responsible for any tax consequences. The dividend payouts from the mutual fund are then taxed at the investor's ordinary income tax bracket.

The discussion, however, gets a little more complex when we turn our attention to capital gains taxes, primarily because there are two categories. We touched on them earlier, but they consist of short-term and long-term capital gains. Capital gains taxes are taxes assessed on the appreciation of the price of a stock when the investor sells that stock. For example, if we bought one share of Coca-Cola for $10, and the next year sold it for $20, we would have to pay tax on that $10 gain. How that $10 gain is taxed depends on how long we held the investment before selling it; this is where the distinction between short-term and long-term capital gains is made.

Short-term capital gains apply to the sale of investments held less than twelve months. These types of gains are taxed just like dividend payments, in that they are taxed at the individual investor's ordinary tax bracket. In our pervious example, if we assume we are in the 28% tax bracket, the $10 gain we had on the share of our Coke stock if we had sold it less than a year after purchase would be taxed at that 28% rate.

Conversely, if we held that investment in Coke stock longer then twelve months and sold it for the same $10 gain, it would fall into the category of long-term capital gains. These types of gains are currently taxed at a flat rate of 15%, regardless of the investor's tax bracket. So that $10 gain would be taxed at 15% and not 28%, obviously an incentive to hold investments for longer then one year. At this current time, long-term capital gains taxes are at an all-time low, encouraging investors to invest and providing them a tax break for holding those investments for at least twelve months. Not too long ago, in the mid to late nineties before President Clinton and his administration began reducing the capital gains rates, the long-term capital gains rate was as high as 33%. These rates are by no means locked in and are subject to change based on the current political and economic environment, so we as investors need to stay appraised of how these changes can affect whether capital gains taxes are likely to rise or fall.

We now know how these different types of capital gains can affect us as individual investors, but now we have to examine how they affect us as mutual fund investors. There are two ways we can incur tax liabilities from owning mutual funds. The first way is if we as individuals pay taxes on the appreciating of our shares in a mutual fund every year. For example, we invest $1,000 into a fund and at some point in the future, that fund appreciates to $2,000, and we redeem our shares in the fund. Then we would pay either short-term or long-term capital gains taxes based on how long we owned the investment. This works the same as if we owned and sold shares of stocks ourselves. It's the second way that we can pay capital gains taxes that can be a little more complex. If the fund manager sells stocks within the fund, those gains have to be passed through to us as the investors. So, when the fund manager sells a stock that has appreciated, then the fund investors realize the tax implications. We knew this, but here is the wrinkle: The capital gains that investors pay is determined by how long the mutual fund held the stock and not how long you or I, as an investor, have owned the fund. It happens frequently that an investor can own a fund for say six months but be responsible for long-term capital gains taxes because the fund manager sold holdings that the fund had held for longer then one year. Now, obviously with the capital gains structure as it is now, this would be beneficial to the investor because they'd only be paying those taxes at the 15% rate, but as we discussed earlier, this may not always be the case because capital gains rates are subject to change. The opposite scenario is also true in that an investor could own a particular fund for several years and still have short-term capital gains tax consequences if the fund sells investments for a gain that they have owned for less than twelve months. In this case, it would be an adverse situation for the investor because the gain would fall under their ordinary income tax bracket and not under the flat 15% long-term rate.

Another scenario that investors have run across, especially in the last few years as the stock market has seen some losses, is when the value of your mutual fund actually drops due to poor performance, and you still receive a tax bill. For example, we invest $1,000 into a fund, and at year's end, the value has dropped to $900. However, the fund sold stocks during the year with built-up capital gains, and, in turn, has to funnel those gains through to us as the investors. So even though we lost money on our investment, we still have to pay those taxes! I know this can seem odd, but it does happen, so be prepared that you could come across a situation like this when investing in certain mutual funds.

Section III - Annuities

Chapter 7 – Introduction

We now come to the section of the book that holds the most mystery for many of us out there: annuities. Not only are they mysterious to most investors because they don't really understand how they work but also because many people don't know when or even if they should own an annuity as part of their investment strategy. Let's dive right in and talk about the very fundamentals of annuities.

Annuities fall into two categories: immediate or deferred. An immediate annuity, for the most part, is very straightforward in that you as the investor give a lump sum of money to an insurance company, and they guarantee to pay you a fixed dollar amount every year for a certain period of time. The period of time is either for your lifetime (or the lifetimes of you and your spouse) or for a designated number of years, referred to as a period certain. This is what is referred to as annuitization, which means your money is not invested in the stock market and earns a small internal rate of return (typically between 2% to 3% depending on how long the annuitization is for) and pays you the fixed income stream over that specified

61

period. Now, if you choose a lifetime pay out, your payments will be based on your life expectancy, based off of the mortality tables published by the IRS every year, and are guaranteed for the rest of your life or the combined lives of you and your spouse, regardless of how long you live. Taking a look at an example, if you purchased an immediate annuity and your life expectancy at the time of purchase is twenty years, that is what your payments will be based on, but if you live thirty years, you still receive those payments for the entire thirty years. Now, on the flip side of that is let's say you only live ten years, then obviously, you haven't received your entire investment back yet, but since you picked a life-only option, your surviving heirs don't receive the balance, but instead, the insurance company keeps it. So it works both ways with this option in that it works in your favor if you outlive your life expectancy, but is detrimental if you pass away prior to reaching that life expectancy number. It's sort of a gamble and is why there is a period certain option available for you to choose as well. The period certain option has nothing to do with how long you are expected to live but simply guarantees you payments for a set number of years. The number of years usually ranges anywhere from five to thirty years and also provides some protection for your heirs. While you may outlive the stream of payments if you choose this option, as would be the case if you chose a ten-year period and lived longer then ten years, if you only lived for five years out of the ten-year period your beneficiaries would receive the balance of the payments.

There are a few more complex options you can choose from such as combining life payments with period certain payments or choosing variable payments every year rather then fixed payments, but that is not a discussion we need to get into at this point. I just want you to have a basic feel for how annuitization works and what some of your options are because it will impact our discussion of the second category of annuities: deferred annuities.

A deferred annuity is a tax-deferred investment vehicle designed primarily to provide an individual or individuals with a stream of income at some point in the future, primarily in retirement. Great, now what does that mean? Remember from our discussion of mutual funds and how they are taxed, I told you that your gains from those funds are taxable to you every year, whether it be as ordinary income from dividends or through capital gains taxes. Think of an annuity as putting a tax deferred blanket over that investment. The gains seen by investors in an annuity AREN'T taxed every year. Those gains are only taxed when the investor takes money out of the annuity. In the year that the investor takes the money out of the annuity contract, they will pay taxes in that year on the amount of earnings they received. These earnings are ALWAYS taxed as ordinary income, and NEVER as capital gains. I'm using capitalization on certain words here to overemphasize this point. The tax-deferred nature of an annuity is the overwhelming factor as to why most people purchase an annuity. There are a few other reasons that we will touch on but the tax-deferral aspect is a concept I want you to always associate with annuities.

There are a few different kinds of deferred annuities with most falling into one of three categories:

1) Variable Annuity
2) Fixed Annuity
3) Index Annuity

I ranked them in order of popularity. I'm going to go into detail on all three types, especially the variable annuity, but I wanted to first give you an idea of the three stacked up against one another. Variable annuities (VAs) are head and shoulders above the other two categories when we look at pure sales numbers. VA sales last year exceeded $100 billion dollars. That's $100 billion dollars. This is an astronomical figure taking into account the fact that if we randomly polled ten people in this country, or the world for that matter, you'd be lucky to find one person who could actually give an explanation of what a VA is and how it works. Fixed and index annuities are also sold quite extensively but don't nearly approach the figures set by VAs for various reasons that we will touch on later in this section.

Annuities are offered by insurance companies throughout the world and are primarily distributed to investors through what are known as broker dealers. Broker dealers are firms of investment representatives licensed with the SEC and NASD to sell investment products to the public. I'm sure you have seen some of the commercials on TV for Merrill Lynch, Morgan Stanley, Dean Witter, Prudential, Citigroup, etc. I'm sure many of you have an investment representative who handles your investment portfolio for you, which may or may not include annuities. The investment representatives at these broker dealer firms sign a selling agreement with the insurance company and then go about selling the various annuities to common investors such as us. They, in turn, get paid a commission by the insurance company on every annuity they sell for that particular company. These commissions are an area I'm going to go into in much greater detail shortly because I believe this to be an area that fosters and breeds the misuse and improper sale of annuities to certain investors.

The leading insurance company in the sale of annuities, particularly VAs, is Hartford Life Insurance. They routinely sell over $20 billion annually in annuities. Other major carriers would be Pacific Life Insurance, Manulife, American Skandia, and ING.

It may seem that I'm off to an ominous start in our discussion of annuities, but I again want to stress that I'm not an annuity basher. The mainstream media and some so-called financial experts who have columns in major newspapers or TV shows on CNBC have strongly expressed their distaste for annuities and think they are generally bad investments. That is simply an uneducated view in my opinion. Are there instances when annuities shouldn't be sold to certain investors? Absolutely. However, there are certain annuities on the market that are reasonably priced and do indeed provide strong benefits and incentives that make sense for some investors. These articles and TV hosts are frequently quoted as proclaiming that annuity costs are too high and investors are always better off simply investing in mutual funds. That is the equivalent of looking at one large-cap mutual fund, seeing annual fees in excess of 1.75%, and declaring that all large-cap funds are too expensive. The fact is, there are annuity products that aren't outrageously expensive and do provide the contract owner with certain benefits, which we will discuss shortly, and these products are worthy of consideration in adding to your portfolio of investments. As I stated, it's been very popular to bash annuities over the last several years, and people love to jump on a bandwagon, but the fact is that annuities, in my opinion, have taken some unjust criticism in the media and aren't the spawn-of-Satan investments that some have made them out to be. That being said, I don't think that annuities, particularly VAs, should be selling at the phenomenally high pace at which they have been selling. There are high-priced, over-hyped products out there being sold by some investment representatives who don't know the first thing about annuities or just don't care if it's right for the client as long as they collect their commissions, and those are the ones you should be careful of. That is why I wanted to write this book, in order to arm you with some good fundamental knowledge of these products so you'll know what the hell you're being sold and whether or not it really is appropriate for you, no matter how persuasive the investment representative's sales pitch may be. That won't matter because you'll be able to ask the right questions, analyze the product, and make your own decision as to whether or not it's the right thing for you.

Chapter 8 - The History of Annuities

As we've talked about, annuities, particularly VAs, have grown in popularity the last few decades to the point where annual VA sales now exceed $200 billion, but annuities are not a new concept. They have actually been in existence for thousands of years. Their history can be traced back to ancient Roman times when they were known as *annua,* which meant "annual stipend" in Latin. Roman citizens could make a one-time payment to the *annua,* and in exchange, receive lifetime payments once a year. This essentially is equivalent to an immediate annuity that we know of today, where an investor pays a lump sum of money to an insurance company and in turn, receives a monthly or annual stream of income for the rest of his or her life.

The use of annuities also gained popularity in seventeenth-century Europe as fundraising vehicles for governments to fund ongoing war campaigns. This time, these vehicles were called *a tontine,* promising to pay citizens for a designated period of time if they invested in the present. England was among the leaders in this practice and created one of the very first group annuities called the State Tontine of 1693 in order to help fund its numerous wars with France. These particular versions of annuities in England added the ability of the owner to assign the annuities to another party, usually by either deed or will, or simply allow them to pass on to other family members, usually children, highlighting another aspect of modern-day annuities in being able to not only provide income for the owner's life but also to pass assets on to family members and provide them with streams of income as well.

Not surprisingly, annuities made their first appearance in America shortly afterwards. In 1759, a company was formed in Pennsylvania for the benefit of Presbyterian ministers and their families. In a similar fashion, the ministers contributed to the fund and then received payments over their lifetime. This same Pennsylvania Company for Insurance on Lives and Granting Annuities was the first company to offer annuities to the general public in 1912. Annuity growth in America over the next few decades was rather slow and didn't really begin to show significant growth until after the stock market crash of 1929 and the ensuing Great Depression. The collapse of the stock market and of the banking system brought to the forefront of the American psyche the concerns over the financial markets and the health of the economy. Consequently, investors started turning to insurance companies because they were viewed as stable companies who specialized in protecting against risk and began to purchase more and more of their products, including annuities. The guarantee of receipt of payments that these annuities offered was exactly the tonic that helped ailing investors' fears during the late 1930's. The New Deal Program introduced by President Roosevelt at this time also helped to benefit the annuity marketplace by encouraging an emphasis on individual investor savings, especially for retirement. In conjunction with this, corporate pension plans began funding group annuities for their employees to help cover the cost of retirement. So, there were several factors that all came together to help promote this marked increase in the popularity of annuities.

Remember our three categories of annuities? Well, these first annuities fell into our category of fixed annuities. Basically, they guaranteed a return of principal, which gave assurance to the shell-shocked investors of the time that in a worst-case scenario they would not lose money. In conjunction, they also typically offered a fixed rate of return the investor would receive while they were contributing to the annuity. Then, when the time arrived for the investor to start drawing income off the annuity, they could elect to receive a fixed amount of income every year for life or for a set number of years if they so chose. The reason for selecting a set number of years and not taking the payments over your lifetime is that the dollar amount of the payments would be higher over a fixed number of years because the insurance company wouldn't have to plan for the contingency that you may live beyond your life expectancy. For example, if a sixty-year-old elects payments for ten years, the insurance company knows exactly how long they have to make those payments. After ten years, the money will be exhausted and that's it. Now, if that same sixty-year-old elects lifetime payments, the amount of those payments will be less because the insurance company doesn't know when he or she is going to pass away. They may live ten years or they may live forty years! If they live to be one hundred, then the insurance company has to pay them accordingly. So that would be the rationale as to why someone may or may not choose to receive payments over their lifetime.

We've already touched on the tax-deferred aspect of annuities and how that is the most attractive feature of an annuity, but the idea of a "guarantee" is also very powerful. You see, investment representatives and financial professionals in general very rarely, if ever, get to use the word guarantee. Since there is always at least some risk associated with investments, this word "guarantee" rarely gets to be used in an ethical manner. If you buy a stock, there is no guarantee it will appreciate in value and there is no guarantee that it won't decrease in value. However, with certain annuities, an investment representative and an insurance company can guarantee that under certain circumstances, you or I as an investor will NOT receive back less than what we put in. That is such a powerful tool in selling annuities, I can't emphasize it enough. Being a part of this business for over five years, I have seen firsthand just how powerful that can be and how many cases it has closed. I'm telling you this because I don't want you to be awed by the word "guarantee." As we delve deeper into this discussion of annuities, you must get full clarification of exactly what is being guaranteed to you. Many investors hear that word and instantly think safety! Those words go off in our heads. We think, "I can't lose any money in this product." That simply is not the case with all annuities, particularly VAs. You CAN lose money in VAs, and not to beat a dead horse here because we are going to revisit this topic throughout this section, but remember to liken insurance companies to casinos. They always hedge their bets, and very rarely, if ever, do they not have the odds stacked in their favor. When you hear the word "guarantee" when discussing an annuity, especially a VA, with an investment representative always ask yourself, "Why are they offering me this guarantee? It must be advantageous for them to do so, and is it really in my best interests?" To expand on the casino analogy, (in case you haven't noticed yet, I do enjoy gambling) it is akin to the casino offering blackjack players insurance. For those of you who might not know what I'm referring to, when the dealer's hand is showing an ace, the players at the table will be offered what is called insurance. The insurance is against the dealer having blackjack[2]. The players can place another bet and take the insurance, and if the dealer does indeed have blackjack, then the player is protected from losing their entire bet. However, if the dealer doesn't have blackjack, the player loses the insurance bet and could lose their original bet if the dealer winds up with a better hand. Blackjack is odds-wise one of the best casino games you can play, because if you play well, the casino's advantage, or house edge, is less then 1%. If you, as a player, take insurance on a given hand, the house edge rises to over 10%! It makes sense because do any of us really think that a casino would offer a player an additional bet in the middle of a hand that was in our favor? Of course not. They are selling you the idea of a guarantee by using the word insurance, when in actuality, it is detrimental to your chances of winning. This is not unlike what insurance companies do with certain types of benefits and riders they offer on some of their annuity products, which we will cover in our discussion on VAs a little later.

[2] The dealer would have blackjack if his 2 cards totaled 21. The ace is worth 11 so any face card (a King, Queen, or Jack, which are worth ten) or a ten would give the dealer blackjack and you as the player would automatically lose.

Speaking of VAs, the first one was created in America in 1952. These contracts varied from their earlier counterparts because they tied the performance to variable subaccounts, which were run similarly to their mutual fund counterparts. So, in essence, investors were investing in tax-deferred mutual fund accounts. Generally, there was no fixed rate of interest guaranteed under these contracts, although a few of them did have fixed subaccounts that offered specified rates of return, so the value of an investor's contract could rise or fall based on the individual subaccounts they chose to invest in. We are going to cover VAs in great detail a little later, but for right now, I just want to make the distinction between them and fixed annuities (FAs) so you can be clear on the difference. VAs are tied to the performance of the market through the subaccounts that the investor can choose while FAs guarantee a specified interest rate the investor will receive for a given time period such as ten years. This makes FAs more attractive to conservative investors due to that magical word "guarantee" while VA's appeal more to investors looking to take some risk and participate in the gains of the stock market.

The growth in popularity of VAs can also be attributed to the explosive growth in mutual funds that we discussed earlier. One fact I think I left out in our mutual fund discussion is that there are twice as many mutual funds as there are stocks for them to buy! As a result, fund managers in the early 1980s began eyeing the growing annuity market as a way to continue to increase their asset base. They created separate subaccounts, which closely mirrored the retail mutual funds they ran, for insurance companies to use for their annuities. This also allowed insurance companies to leverage the star power of mutual fund money managers to sell their annuities if they could advertise that a certain manager was also managing money for any of the subaccounts within their product. It really was a mutually beneficial arrangement for both the insurance companies and the fund managers, and it is an arrangement that is stronger than ever today.

Chapter 9 - Variable Annuities

This section is really the "meat" of this book, and it's why I chose to put it ahead of both fixed and index annuities. We will talk about both of those products but VAs and how they operate was the driving force behind writing this book, and I want to get right into it. As I stated earlier, the VA marketplace has been growing at a fantastic rate over the last decade and now annually tops $200 billion in sales. There are several reasons for this, but the most prevalent one is the dedication and the resources that insurance companies have devoted to growing these sales figures. VAs are wildly profitable for insurance companies, and once this fact was discovered, they ramped up their sales forces and really hit the pavement to boost their sales figures, and thus far, they've done a fantastic job. I've likened insurance companies to casinos, and here is a perfect illustration of that point. Let's say a casino puts a new type of slot machine onto its gaming floor and that machine becomes instantly popular and starts to generate eye-popping profits, much like the Wheel of Fortune slot machines have done in recent years. I'm sure any of us who have been in a casino in the last five years have seen the Wheel of Fortune machines and seen them prominently displayed because according to recent figures, it is far and away the most successful and profitable slot machine ever produced! So the casinos, of course, make these machines readily accessible and fill their floor with as many as they can. Think of VAs as these new, hot slot machines, generating tremendous profits for insurance companies. Wouldn't it make sense to thrust the entire force of their sales and marketing departments behind these products? Of course it would. That is exactly what has taken place. It makes all the sense in the world because insurance companies, such as Hartford which has been in existence since 1810, have recognizable brand names and already have tens of thousands of people who have some type of insurance with them, be it fire, auto, life, etc. There is already an established client base that recognizes and trusts that brand name. We are going to cover exactly why VAs are so profitable, and when we do, you will see why, recently, there have been more and more state suitability regulations put forth in regards to the selling of some of these products.

I want to make my position very clear once again before we delve into this discussion. I have worked for insurance companies for five plus years selling and analyzing these products, and I think, for the most part, they can be good investment vehicles. I'm not of the opinion, as some pundits are, that annuities in general and especially VAs are always poor investments. That simply is not the case. There are annuities on the market that are reasonably priced, offer a wide range of investment choices, and act as a nice compliment to round out an investor's portfolio. What I'm here to warn you about, ladies and gentlemen, are the annuities, mostly VAs, that tack on extra fees for options that you simply don't need and, in most cases, are being conned into buying by investment representatives and insurance companies preying on your fears. Fear is a powerful motivational factor, and when you apply fear to money, it instantly peaks an investor's curiosity and gets you or me wondering...."My goodness...could that scenario really happen?" Right there, that is the sales hook! The living benefits offered by insurance companies that we are going to discuss are predicated squarely on that fear. These benefits will offer you protection against the absolute worst-case scenario that could happen, and since the odds of that scenario actually occurring are so minute, the insurance companies simply sit back and reap the profits. When you hear the words bonus, living benefit, principal protection, etc. be aware that they are merely eye candy to grab your attention and tack on unnecessary fees and expenses to the VA you are about to purchase. Insurance companies in this way are no different from any other company in the world, they are simply trying to generate revenues and increase profits, and we shouldn't judge them too harshly for that. Where I take exception, and why I felt a book such as this needed to be written, is that the facts about these products simply aren't widely known or understood by the general public. You and I as investors are being taken advantage of in a lot of cases because we simply are uneducated or worse—misinformed as to what we are actually purchasing.

As I stated earlier, this is somewhat of a trickle-down effect because the investment representatives selling these products often either don't understand what they are selling and consequently, mislead their clients, or they simply don't care to understand the products and just want to know how to sell them effectively and collect the commissions. It is very hard for an investor to get accurate information about a particular product from a source other then their investment representative. Yes, they can read the prospectus that by law must accompany the sale of a VA, but attempting to read through the legalese wording in that document and make sense out of it is often equivalent to trying to decipher ancient Egyptian hieroglyphs! Not to mention, it's incredibly boring and tedious to do so. Well, what about the client service teams that investors can call for information at the insurance company? I'm going to let you in on a secret here, the client services teams at insurance companies, and I'm talking about all insurance companies with regards to VAs, are mediocre at best. Now, this is not their fault. I don't blame the individuals manning these call centers at all. I've worked hand in hand with them my entire career, but they're not given the chance to excel at their jobs. The turnover rate in these call centers is extremely high, usually turning over about half their staff every twelve months, so the majority of people working there never get the experience they need to fully understand the nuances of the products.

There is a great deal of information a person must know in order to fully understand a wide range of annuity products, as you are going to see when we finish with this section, and the people in these call centers simply don't get the time needed for that. The turnover rate is generally so high because they are vastly underpaid for what they do. Most insurance companies start off a call center employee making anywhere from $20,000 to $25,000 per year. That is pre-tax. This is all insurance companies, and any company that tells you differently is flat out lying to you. You want to know why they pay so little? They, being the insurance companies, don't value it as a high priority. That is the bottom line. If they did, they would pay higher salaries in order to keep the best and brightest on those phones to help their clients understand how their annuity works. When speaking to you as an investor, the company will tell you how much they value their customer service, but once they have your investment dollars in their products, it simply isn't a priority any longer. They want to gather new assets and would rather pay the money to their wholesaling staff and sales managers than to the customer service division. The insurance company already has your money, and for you to get out of that contract, you will be paying a CDSC, just as if you were in a B-share mutual fund, and any bonus you received when you started the contract will likely be charged back, so the insurance company has already made their money off of you. Insurance companies' goals are to gather new assets, and that is what they allocate their time, money, and resources to doing.

Before we discuss some of the benefits and reasons for buying a VA, I want to just go over again exactly what a VA is and how it is structured. A VA is, at its core, a tax-deferred mutual fund with certain guarantees upon the death of the contract owner. The investor and their investment representative choose from an array of mutual funds, called subaccounts, within the VA and their contract value fluctuates up and down based on the performance of these subaccounts. We're going to discuss the guarantees upon the investor's death in the very next section, but I want you to keep in mind that idea of a tax-deferred mutual fund. The investor purchasing the VA is, in most cases, the owner of the contract. I say in most cases because there are times when a trust or some other entity can own the contract, but for our purposes, we are going to assume that they are the owner. The owner has all the rights to the contract; so they can determine investment options, make withdrawals, etc. Now, on the contract, there is also someone called the annuitant. The annuitant has no rights to the contract in any way, although this tends not to matter because in most cases the owner and the annuitant are the same person. If the contract were to be annuitized[3], it would be based on the annuitant's age at the time. The final name(s) on the contract is that of the beneficiary or beneficiaries if there is more than one. The beneficiary is the person who receives the death benefit if the owner passes away. The majority of the time, the beneficiary is a spouse, the children, or other family members. There is no limit to how many beneficiaries can be listed on a contract, and in the vast majority of cases, they have no rights to the contract either.

---

3 Annuitization refers to the guaranteed payments an insurance company makes to an individual for a designated period of time. It will be covered in greater detail in a future chapter

Chapter 10 - The Reasons to Purchase a Variable Annuity

Death Benefit

The primary reason for an investor to buy a VA is for the guaranteed death benefit. This is a feature that mutual funds, stocks, bonds, or other investment vehicles simply can't offer. In essence, it guarantees an investor that upon his or her death, a certain dollar amount will pass on to his or her beneficiary. In most cases, the minimum guarantee in the contract is the current contract value or a return of the premiums invested in the contract. Let's take a look at a quick example of an initial investment of $10,000 to clarify just how this would work.

Year	Initial Investment	Contract Value	Death Benefit
0	$10,000	$10,000	$10,000
1	$10,000	$12,000	$12,000
2	$10,000	$15,000	$15,000
3	$10,000	$8,000	$10,000

As you can see, the initial investment stays level at $10,000, as we assume no additional payments into the contract. Notice that the death benefit never drops below that original $10,000, even at the end of year three, when our contract value drops from $15,000 to $8,000 because of the losses experienced within the investment sub-accounts. So, if you as the owner of the contract were to pass away at the end of year three, your designated beneficiary would receive $10,000 instead of just $8,000. This is the essence of what VAs offer investors when compared to other investment vehicles such as mutual funds. It is a form of insurance on your investment without actually being life insurance. The advantage of the VA here is that it requires no medical exam, so the health of the investor doesn't factor into whether they can or can't buy the contract as it would if they were applying for life insurance. The disadvantage is that the earnings from the VA when they pass to the beneficiary are only tax-deferred and not tax-free as they would be under a life insurance policy. Any gains realized under the contract would be taxable to the beneficiary as ordinary income in the year they are received. All taxable distributions from annuities are always taxed as ordinary income at the recipient's tax bracket and never as capital gains. This is another important difference between annuities and mutual funds. One of the arguments recently used against investing in annuities is that since long-term capital gains rates are at an all-time low right now at 15%, it makes sense for investors to invest in mutual funds because of the tax savings of only having to pay 15% long-term capital gains taxes versus ordinary income taxes which could be as high as 39.6% on annuities for investors in the highest tax bracket. There are two flaws in this argument, and they are that the owner or beneficiary only pays the taxes on annuities when they actually realize the gains. By that I mean if you or I own an annuity and watch our initial investment of say $10,000 continue to appreciate year after year, we would not pay any taxes on those gains until we withdrew them from the contract. In this way, we can determine when and how much of a tax burden we must be responsible for in any given year because until we actually realize the gains, meaning we physically receive the money, our investment continues to grow tax-deferred. Remember that with mutual funds this is not the case. The appreciations on our mutual funds are taxable to us each year even though we didn't realize any of the gains. For example, if the fund we own continues to appreciate year after year, we are still responsible for the taxes, either from dividends or capital gains, even though we haven't physically received any of the gains yet. Remember that earlier we discussed how the capital gains rates have fluctuated over the years and that the low rates we are currently experiencing are by no means guaranteed in the future.

The example we just reviewed is often referred to as a standard death benefit offered on VAs. Many times, the death benefits have enhanced features that either come with the product or can be elected upon purchase. The most common of these enhancements is usually referred to as a step-up feature. You'll also hear it referred to as a high-water mark, a ratchet, or lock-in feature. Whatever the name, it accomplishes the same thing, and that is to guarantee a death benefit for the investor that can be higher than just the value of the contract at the time of death. Let's take a look at our previous example and add the feature to see how it works.

Year	Investment	Contract Value	Death Benefit	Step-Up Feature
0	$10,000	$10,000	$10,000	$10,000
1	$10,000	$12,000	$12,000	$12,000
2	$10,000	$15,000	$15,000	$15,000
3	$10,000	$8,000	$10,000	**$15,000**

The benefit of the feature is highlighted above. From our earlier example showing the standard death benefit, the fourth column shows that the death benefit is equal to the original $10,000 we invested in the contract three years earlier. Now, move over to the last column and we can see that with the step-up feature the death benefit payout to the beneficiary under this same scenario is $15,000. That $15,000 came as a result of our contract value at the end of year two. The step-up feature locks in the contract value at the end of every contract year as our minimum guaranteed death benefit. So, since we had this feature on our contract, even though the contract value dropped from $15,000 to $8,000, our guaranteed death benefit stays at $15,000. This is a key selling point of VAs and does make them attractive investment alternatives. Obviously, there is a cost associated with this type of feature, and we are going to go over all of the fees and charges associated with VAs a little later. The big advantage here is that it helps to protect the investor's gains within the contract. So, if the stock market does drop, as it has the last few years, the beneficiaries of the contract, most often a spouse or children, receive that highest lock-in amount as a death benefit. With mutual funds and other types of investments, that is not the case as the surviving beneficiaries would simply receive current value as of the date of death. Since nobody knows exactly when they are going to die, it protects the investor from having the unfortunate luck of dying at the wrong time and ensures that their heirs will reap the benefits of any gains previously realized within the contract.

The other enhancement that has gained popularity over recent years is called a roll-up feature. The roll-up feature guarantees the investor that their death benefit will increase by a certain percent no matter how their underlying investments perform. The percent increase generally ranges anywhere from between 3% to 7% and typically stops rolling up when the owner hits a certain age or the roll-up feature reaches a certain dollar amount. Again, let's revisit our example to get an idea of how this feature works; we're assuming a roll-up feature of 5%.

Year	Investment	Contract Value	Step-Up	Roll-Up
0	$10,000	$10,000	$10,000	$10,000
1	$10,000	$12,000	$12,000	$10,500
2	$10,000	$12,000	$12,000	$11,025
3	$10,000	$8,000	$12,000	$11,576
4	$10,000	$10,000	$12,000	**$12,155**

In the last column, you can see the 5% roll-up feature, and to re-enforce how this feature operates, I extended the example out another year and reduced the step-up feature from $15,000 to $12,000. So our original $10,000 investment continues to lock-in at the end of each contract year via the step-up feature but also compounds on itself at 5% through the roll-up feature. In most VA products, both of these features, the step-up and the roll-up, come packaged together. The majority of products will offer the step-up feature as a stand-alone option, but if the roll-up feature is selected, it generally comes with the step-up feature, so you get the higher of the two for a death benefit. I said that the $10,000 compounds on itself for the roll-up feature and that is an important aspect to understand because there can easily be confusion when you say the death benefit is going to roll-up by at least 5% every year. We see that after the first contract year, our step-up feature is at $12,000 and that stays level at $12,000 at the end of year 2 because our contract value didn't increase. The $12,000 stayed level and didn't increase by 5%. The roll-up feature after the first year increased by 5% to $10,500 and that $10,500 rolled up by 5% the next year to $11,025, but had no effect on the step-up feature. This is where some investors can get confused because their minimum death benefit after the first year is $12,000, so oftentimes, they expect that $12,000 will roll-up by the 5% guaranteed the following year and that is not the case. These two features work independently of one another, and upon death, the beneficiary would receive the higher of the two options or the contract value if that is a higher amount. That being said, after the fourth year, we can see that the 5% roll-up feature has passed the step-up feature and is higher then the current contract value, which is $10,000. So, if the contract owner were to pass away at the end of year 4, their beneficiaries would receive $12,155. Another point I want to mention here is that the roll-up percent, whatever it may be, is net of fees[4]. I know we haven't discussed the fee structure yet, but when we do, I want you to keep that in mind. This is an appealing feature to investors, particularly to more conservative investors, because it gives them a guaranteed return on their investment. I'll emphasize the point once again how powerful using the word "guarantee" is in trying to sell an investment product to an investor. It has become even that much more important with the current political and economic environment. Even though there is already a guarantee in the VA that, at minimum, the investor's beneficiaries will get back at least the $10,000 they originally invested, people in general don't like to see their investments just stay flat! Rightly so, because with inflation increasing historically at a rate of 3%, the buying power of their money is decreasing. In essence, it is like going broke very slowly, which is unfortunately what happens to many common investors who keep the bulk of their money invested in CDs or just in savings accounts. When an investment representative can use the word guarantee when discussing a VA product, it is exactly what a lot of investors want to hear. Although the guarantee is on the death benefit and not on the contract value, so to fully realize the benefit, the investor would have to die, it gives them peace of mind knowing that the proceeds paid to their beneficiaries will, at worst, likely keep pace with inflation.

In my opinion, these death benefits are the true driving force behind an investor owning a VA. In its purest state, with no additional riders or benefits that we will discuss next, the VA offers you or I this certain protection that no other investment vehicle, with the exception of life insurance, can offer. Used in this way, VAs are a wonderful compliment to an investor's portfolio of investments. They allow you or me to set aside a set amount of money that will pass on to our heirs guaranteed, with no chance of loss due to market fluctuations.

4 Net of Fees means that the benefit on the contract will increase by the designated percent, in this case 5%, regardless of the contract charges. For example, if the charges were 2% the benefit would still increase by 5% and not 3%(5%-2%).

Living Benefits

The fraudulent sales of VAs that I have alluded to thus far are without a doubt due to the proliferation of living benefits. Living benefits work in many ways like death benefits, except rather than guaranteeing a payout upon the death of the owner, they offer guarantees during the owner's life. These types of benefits have gained mass popularity in recent years for two reasons. The first is that it allows insurance companies to collect extra fees and charges on the contracts, thus making them more profitable. The second reason is that they make the sale of VAs easier for investment representatives. Now, rather than the sales pitch being confined to offering guaranteed benefits to the owner's heirs, the investment representatives can offer guarantees to the owner during their lifetime and to their beneficiaries upon their death. You see, that just opened up a whole new group of investors to market to. There are many investors with a good deal of money out there whose primary concern is not to pass on money to their ultimate heirs but to protect their assets for their own use and consumption. Either they have no real family to whom they may pass on the assets or they have strained relationships with their existing family and/or friends and could care less about leaving them a dime. Speaking from experience, and I think many of you can relate to this, family squabbles happen frequently, and all too often, those squabbles unfortunately settle around money. That's because money and family just don't mix. In an ideal world, they would be kept completely separate and that would alleviate a great deal of the tension that strains family relationships, but unfortunately, we don't live in an ideal world, so we have to face the reality of that situation.

Once this new market was discovered, insurance companies raced to introduce these living benefits onto their product lines, develop sales pitches for the investment representatives to use with their clients, and reap the profits.

Again, I refer back to the analogy of insurance companies and casinos. When developing these new living benefits, the insurance companies are very careful to have their actuaries, who are very bright people, stack the odds in their favor through the terms and pricing of these living riders. How does that old saying go:

"If it sounds too good to be true, then it probably is."

How accurate a statement that is! The benefits that we are going to cover in this section sound wonderful, until you really look at what you are paying for. In some cases, you are paying for protection against something that has never happened, NEVER happened since 1929! Yet people are buying protection against it at a significant cost. Keep in mind what I said earlier as you read this section: these benefits, for the most part, are preying on your worst fears, and insurance companies know that uneducated investors will buy them whether we need them or not. Some of you may feel insulted by that, and to some extent you should, but it's not saying that you are dumb or stupid. You just haven't been educated as to what to look for and what questions to ask, and the insurance companies know this. In most cases, these living benefits have several moving parts, as you'll see when we examine a few of them, and the investment representatives, who have years of training and certifications in the financial arena, don't fully understand them. Throughout my career, I have talked with countless investment representatives who had a total misconception as to what benefits they sold their client. If these individuals can't fully grasp the inner workings of each benefit, then how are common investors, the majority of whom have no financial training or background at all, going to understand them? The answer is you're not, and quite frankly, that is what insurance companies count on. There are really three types of living benefits that dominate the marketplace today, and I want to give you a basic understanding of how each works, what investors they are designed for, and what questions to ask if you are ever presented the opportunity to purchase one. They can be somewhat complex, and I don't want to delve into every possible scenario that can occur with each one because it would make the book several hundred pages long! As with everything in my writing, I want you to understand the fundamentals of what they are guaranteeing and generally how much each rider costs so you can internalize the information and be armed with the knowledge to ask the right questions to help you make your decision.

Principal Protection

This benefit is probably the most straightforward, and in most cases, the one benefit you should never select. Each company puts their own particular wrinkle on this benefit, but basically, it guarantees that the original amount you invested in the contract, we'll continue to use our example of $10,000, will be guaranteed over a certain number of years. For example, say we invest our $10,000 today, and ten years from now, if we have lost money and our contract value is $8,000, the insurance company will deposit $2,000 into our account in order to make us whole again, back to our original investment of $10,000. Basically, no matter how poorly our subaccounts perform, we are guaranteed not to lose any money over that ten-year period. Virtually all benefits fitting this description are for ten-year time frames for a very good reason. Since 1929, the year of the stock market crash that we spoke of earlier, there has never, NEVER been any ten-year period where the S&P 500 Index has lost money. That is seventy-five years, and in no ten-year period in those seventy-five years would you have lost money if you were simply invested in an S&P 500 Index account. Over those seventy-five years, this country has experienced a World War, several smaller wars, a great depression, a presidential assassination, terrorist attacks, vast budget deficits, and a host of other adversities, and yet, never has the S&P Index been down over any ten-year period during that time. What could the country experience in the future that would make that happen? I can't think of anything, and that doesn't mean it's not possible. Anything is possible. It's possible that I could be elected president of the United States, not very likely, but possible. You see what I'm driving at here? This is a worst-case, catastrophic scenario that is being laid before you. I can also guarantee you that the insurance companies are well aware of these facts, and it's the precise reason they choose a ten-year time frame! They've hedged their bets, just like a casino would, and they collect their fees for offering protection against an event that has never happened.

The sales pitch you will hear for purchasing this kind of rider is related to insurance. The pitch goes something like this:

> You buy insurance for you car. You buy insurance for your house against fire and water damage. You buy insurance on your life. Why shouldn't you buy insurance on your assets as well?

I love this one. The pitch is correct. We do buy insurance for our cars, houses, and on our lives, but there is a very good reason for this. People get in car accidents by the hundreds every day. People lose their houses to fire damage and other natural disasters every day. People die every day! If there hadn't been a car accident in this country for the last seventy-five years, how many people would purchase car insurance? My guess on this one is NONE. Laws stating that you must have car insurance also wouldn't exist. If there hadn't been a single death in the country for seventy-five years, do you think people would be increasing the amount of life insurance they owned? Of course not. My point is that these occurrences that the insurance companies and their sales forces make analogies to happen every day, but the event they are offering protection against hasn't occurred once in seventy-five years. This is the kind of information that is not widely known to the general investing public but is crucial to making an informed decision. On the surface, it sounds like an attractive offer; however, when we look beneath the surface, we see that it's not a suitable rider for the vast majority of annuity investors. The only investors this particular rider should appeal to are the high-risk investors who are looking to invest in the most aggressive subaccounts they can. In essence, they are looking to hit home runs by investing in small-cap growth accounts, highly concentrated sector funds, or any other high-risk, high-reward fund they can find. This rider would allow them to do just that under a tax-deferred umbrella with a guarantee that if none of these aggressive investments panned out, they would know that they would receive their original investment back. However, most insurance companies don't offer a wide array of high-risk investment choices in their annuities, and if a rider such as this is selected, the investor is usually required to invest in one of a number of pre-packaged investment portfolios. This means that the insurance company, not the investor, chooses how the money will be invested for the ten years, and oftentimes, this can't be changed by the investor or they risk losing their guarantee protection. Basically, when you purchase the contract, the insurance company already knows into which subaccounts you'll be investing and can take precautions to hedge their position against any losses you might encounter over that guarantee period. Not to mention the fact that aggressive investors such as these most often don't have ten-year time horizons. They're not long-term investors. Their goal is typically to turn over their investments within a few years, or in some cases, a few months, take the profit and invest in the next hot fund or investment they can find. This fact is ultimately the reason they don't purchase annuities in the first place. So, if we eliminate this group of investors, I can't really think of any investor who should purchase this type of living rider. If your goal is investing for the long-term in a well-diversified portfolio of subaccounts within your VA, then there is no basis for purchasing this feature.

However, let's take a look at a scenario, and we will give the insurance companies the benefit of the doubt and say that over a ten-year period the S&P 500 Index was down 10%. This is a scenario that has never happened, but for illustrative purposes, we'll assume that it has. Now, if we invested our $10,000 into an S&P 500 Index account in our VA and chose a principal protection rider, we increased our expenses by roughly 65 basis points. We'll also assume that our account stayed flat at $10,000 for the first nine years and right before the end of our tenth year, there was a sharp drop of 10%. At the end of our guarantee period, our account value is now worth only $9,000 due to the 10% decline, so the insurance company makes us whole again to our original investment amount of $10,000. This worked out well. We had the opportunity to invest in the market for ten years, and although we lost money, we still got our $10,000 back. As Columbo would say when he's about to solve the mystery, "Excuse me, I just have one more question." My question to you is, "What did we wind up paying for that rider?" Some simple math shows us that .65% off of $10,000 is $65 per year. Multiply that by 10 and we come out with $650. That changes things about because that means $650 of the $1,000 that the insurance company paid us was our own money! You see, without those extra fees, every year our account would have actually gained money, and not stayed flat because remember that $10,000 that stayed flat was net of all fees. So we really only got back $350 from the insurance company, and when you factor in the time value of money and inflationary pressures, that $350 gain is probably worthless in terms of real spending power. Again, I ask, "What are you paying for?" Even if the scenario of a 10% drop in the S&P 500 occurs, isn't the insurance company basically just giving you your fees back? That is money they have charged you over that ten-year time frame, and if they used the money from those fees wisely, they have paid for that $350 expense many, many times over. Now you're armed with the knowledge you need about this particular kind of rider to ask the right questions and make an informed decision.

Typically, the expense for this rider ranges anywhere from about .60% to .75% for a ten-year protection rider. There are a few products out on the market that do offer shorter protection periods, down to seven years, but their expenses would be upwards of 1.5%. Revisiting our talk on mutual funds, we know that an increase of even 20 or 30 basis points can have a significant impact on our returns, so as I just showed in that example, you can well imagine the impact that 60 to 75 basis points would have.

Income Benefit

This benefit has more of a practical use then the principal protection rider we just discussed, but it still requires quite a bit of probing to determine if it's suitable for your needs or not. Essentially, this rider guarantees the investor the right to, at some point in the future, annuitize their contract and guarantee a fixed income stream for the rest of their lives. Remember from an earlier footnote, that annuitizing a contract moves it from the category of a deferred annuity to an immediate annuity. The contract ceases to participate in the market at the time of annuitization and begins to provide the owner with a stream of income. Usually, if a contract is annuitized, it is done so based on the current contract value. However, these particular riders allow you or me to annuitize off of an amount they refer to as the benefit base. The benefit base, at a minimum, will increase by a certain percent every year, typically between 5% to 7%, regardless of how the underlying subaccounts perform. Let's take a quick look at an example:

Year	Initial Investment	Contract Value	Benefit Base (5%)
0	$10,000	$10,000	$10,000
1	$10,000	$12,000	$10,500
2	$10,000	$15,000	$11,025
3	$10,000	$8,000	$11,576
4	$10,000	$11,000	$12,155
5	$10,000	$13,000	$12,762
6	$10,000	$15,000	$13,400
7	$10,000	$14,000	$14,071
8	$10,000	$15,000	$14,774
9	$10,000	$12,000	$15,513
10	$10,000	$15,000	$16,288

You can see that the benefit base has been growing at 5% each year as the contract value has fluctuated. The general holding time on this kind of rider is ten years, meaning that to take advantage of the rider and be able to annuitize at the higher benefit base, you would need to wait at least ten years before annuitizing. This works in much the same manner as the roll-up feature on the death benefit, except that the benefit is payable during the owner's lifetime.

Another feature of the death benefit that is also generally included in these income riders is the step-up feature. The benefit base of the income rider would be the higher of the step-up feature or the roll-up feature. Let's take another look at our previous example to see how this actually works:

Year	Contract Value	Step-Up	Roll-Up (5%)	Benefit Base
0	10,000	10,000	$10,000	$10,000
1	12,000	12,000	$10,500	$12,000
2	15,000	15,000	$11,025	$15,000
3	$8,000	15,000	$11,576	$15,000
4	11,000	15,000	$12,155	$15,000
5	13,000	15,000	$12,762	$15,000
6	15,000	15,000	$13,400	$15,000
7	14,000	15,000	$14,071	$15,000
8	15,000	15,000	$14,774	$15,000
9	12,000	15,000	$15,513	$15,513
10	15,000	15,000	$16,288	$16,288

Here we see that the last column, the benefit base column, is the higher of either the step-up or roll-up features. Again, this is virtually identical to the death benefit scenario we went over earlier, except that this is a benefit designed to provide the owner of the contract an income stream during their lifetime.

The expense for this kind of rider varies from insurance company to insurance company; however, the general range is somewhere between .60% and .75%. Generally, it is not anymore expensive than the principal protection rider, which was the first living rider we discussed, but there is a difference on how the expenses are charged. Usually, with this kind of income rider, the annual expense of .60% to .75% is charged off the benefit base or the contract value, whichever is higher. This is vital information for you to be aware of because very often, unless you ask this question or read the prospectus, you won't be made aware of it. Yes, it will be disclosed in small print on sales literature you receive or on a hypothetical illustration that may get worked up for you, but it will not be volunteered to you by the investment representative or insurance company. The investment representative may not even be aware of it, or more likely, will not volunteer the information to you in fear of losing the sale. The insurance company, on the other hand, goes through all the proper disclosures required by the NASD and SEC, but they know that the majority of investors don't read all the small print on the sales litera-ture, and even if they did, they more than likely haven't been edu-cated to understand what the term "benefit base" means. This isn't a deceptive practice because, let's face it, no sales-based industry just volunteers information to customers that they think would jeopar-dize the sale, and the fact of the matter is that responsibility must lie with the customer to investigate and understand what it is they are buying. That's the reason I felt so strongly about writing this book. I wanted to give common investors the knowledge to make informed investment decisions when it came to mutual funds and annuities.

Now, back to the business of expenses. If we look at the example above and see that at the end of year 3, our benefit base is $15,000 while our contract value is only $8,000, that means the .60% to .75% charged to us for this rider is based off of $15,000! Even though that money is not tangible in your hands, meaning that if you were to end the contract, you would only receive $8,000, you are still being charged as if it were $15,000. This is one of the ways that insurance companies again hedge their bets with these sorts of living riders. The actuaries have already done the modeling and have priced the riders accordingly. Between the fees they collect off the benefit base and ability they have to reinvest that money back into the company to grow and expand their business, they have already paid for the living benefit you are receiving many times over and have reaped a very healthy profit. Also, keep in mind that to receive the full benefit of this rider, you or I must annuitize the contract, so the insurance company doesn't pay the benefit base to us in one lump sum but rather a portion of it every year over our lifetime or a set number of years. So if we add up the ten years we must wait before we could even annuitize, and let's say the twenty years it would take for us to receive the whole benefit base through those annual annuity pay-ments, that gives us a time horizon of roughly thirty years. The insurance companies know this, and they know that by collecting those additional fees every year and not having to repay the entire benefit base for thirty years or so, they can make a fortune.

With all that being said, I do think there are some investors who could benefit from this particular rider. Unlike the principal protection riders, I do believe that in certain cases these riders can be useful. The investor needing a guaranteed fixed income when they retire to supplement their income can benefit from this. With the roll-up feature, they can be assured of a minimum amount they will be able to receive ten years from now, with the potential of it being more due to the step-up feature, and they can plan accordingly. That being said, I don't believe that this feature is suitable for the majority of investors, and here are the reasons why:

Reason number one is that VA contracts after ten years are going to be free of CDSC. Thus the investors can withdrawal money from their contract, as they need without giving up control. By giving up control, I mean that once a contract is annuitized the contract owner no longer has control over the investment options or the amount of withdrawals. You, as the investor, are going to receive the same amount of income every year whether you need it or not. In addition, once you annuitize, the contract no longer is invested in the subaccounts and loses the potential for continued growth[5]. Once you notify the insurance company that you want to annuitize, they begin the pay out phase of the contract, and your money gets removed from the subaccounts and earns an internal rate of return that generally ranges between about 2% to 3% based on your age. It is one of the reasons that representatives in the insurance industry refer to annuitization as "annuicide," because the investor is, in essence, killing their contract. Our example earlier discussed receiving income over a twenty-year time period, after we annuitize, which means that for those twenty years after annuitization, we earn a 2% to 3% rate of return on our investment. That isn't even enough to keep pace with the historical rate of inflation. If we give the insurance companies the benefit of the doubt and assume that the stock market performs poorly over the ten-year period that our money is invested in the

5 There is an option called variable annuitization that some insurance companies do offer. In this case your annuitization amount would stay invested in the subaccounts and your payments would fluctuate every year based on their performance. Not elected in most cases because the payments aren't guaranteed.

subaccounts and we annuitize at the 5% roll-up base and we earn an internal rate of return of 3% for twenty years once we annuitize, that means for the thirty years the insurance company had our money, we earned less then 4% per year! Does that sound so wonderful as to pay the extra .60% to .75% for? When you think in those terms, it certainly takes the luster off of these types of benefits. On the other hand, by keeping the contract in force and not annuitizing, you keep control. If you need to take money out one year, then you simply take a withdrawal; if you don't need to, you leave the money in the contract to stay invested in the subaccounts and keep growing tax-deferred. Maybe some years, you need more money then what your annuitization payout would have been, and some years, you might not need any additional income at all. The point is, you keep control, and you keep the flexibility of when and where to take money from your contract. That is the primary reason that the vast majority of VA contracts, well over 80%, never get annuitized! It's one of the great ironies of annuities, that one of their original designs was to, at one point, provide the owner with a guaranteed stream of income for life, but four out of five VA contract owners never exercise that right, the reason being that they don't want to give up control of their contract. This helps lead me into my second reason.

Reason number two is that a ten-year time frame is a long time for any investor to know exactly what their financial situation will be like after those ten years. You may need to end the contract after five years; you may find out that you really don't need to supplement your retirement income after all and are paying fees for a rider you'll never use; or like most investors, you will not want to relinquish control of your contract after ten years and just decide to take withdrawals to supplement your income. Whatever the scenario may be, the fact is that most annuity contracts never get annuitized so statistics suggest that many of the people purchasing these types of riders will never exercise them.

Reason number three is that the guarantee amount of 5% to 7% that insurance companies are offering you is below the historical average returns of the S&P 500, which is a little over 10%. A conservative, well-diversified investor can reasonably expect to earn between

7% and 10% per year over a ten-year or longer time horizon, so what exactly are you paying for? The guarantee roll-up figures are the very bottom end of what conservative, risk-averse investors, which compose the majority of VA contract owners, can expect in annual returns over that time period anyway, so that roll-up feature in most cases will never come into play. Now, the step-up feature is a good feature on these riders because of potential year-to-year volatility some of the subaccounts could experience. However, remember that the charge for the rider will be charged to that high lock-in value so you do pay a hefty price for that protection.

In general, I'm not a supporter of these types of riders, but as I've said, there is a small segment of investors out there who could benefit from the income security they provide. The questions you need to ask yourself when presented with a rider such as this are:

1) What are my financial goals ten years from now?

2) Am I going to need a guaranteed, fixed amount of income to supplement me in retirement?

3) Do I want to give up control of my investment at some point to guarantee that income?

If the answers to questions 2 and 3 are yes, then you should perhaps consider an income rider such as this and begin to shop around for the best-priced rider you can find. Then, when you've done that, the final question you must ask yourself is:

4) Do I believe that the benefits I'm going to receive in ten years outweigh the expenses I'm going to pay during those ten years?

Unfortunately, there are no stock answers for these questions. I wish there were, but it really is an individual decision that is unique to every investor. All you can do is arm yourself with as much knowledge as possible and use that to sort through the different investment options and see if any of them suits your particular needs.

Withdrawal Benefit

A withdrawal benefit also guarantees the owner income but doesn't require annuitization. So you or I, as the owner, don't have to give up control of the contract in order to receive the benefits of the rider. In that way, it is different from the income rider, but both riders do provide for a guaranteed income stream, they just accomplish it in different ways. The withdrawal benefit rider guarantees income to the owner through a series of withdrawals from the contract. Just as if the owner decided they needed to draw funds from their contract and requested a withdrawal, the same process applies here. However, there are limits as to the number of withdrawals the owner would receive every year. The way most of these riders read, they guarantee a certain percentage of the account value, usually between 5% to 7%, to be withdrawn every year until the account is exhausted. It guarantees that if you or I invested $10,000 into a VA and elected this rider, at a minimum, we would be guaranteed to receive the entire $10,000 back through these series of withdrawals even if the value of our contract reached zero. I know that probably sounds very confusing right now, but let's take a look at an example that will help to clarify what exactly the rider does:

Year	Contract Value	Withdrawals (7%)	Withdrawal Account
1	$10,000	$0	$10,000
2	$8,000	$700	$9,300
3	$5,000	$700	$8,600
4	$3,000	$700	$7,900
5	$0	$700	$7,200
6	$0	$700	$6,500
7	$0	$700	$5,800
8	$0	$700	$5,100

Let's take a look at each column in the above example and define exactly what they represent. The contract value is the actual dollar amount we invested in the contract, and as you can see, it declines rapidly in this example and hits $0 in year 5. The withdrawal column shows the 7% withdrawal that you, as the contract owner, would receive every year. You can see it stays steady at $700 per year be-cause the 7% is based off of the original $10,000 investment. The final column is the withdrawal account column, which begins at the initial investment level of $10,000 and gets reduced subsequently by $700 per year. This is really the scenario that the insurance compa-nies want you to see because it truly shows the benefits of the rider. As you can see, the contract value is depleted at the end of year 5, and under normal circumstances, that would signal the end of the contract, but not in this case. Your contract has technically termi-nated; however, since you elected the withdrawal benefit rider, it has moved into what is referred to as the payout phase. You can see from the above example that even though there is no longer any money in the contract, you continue to receive a check for $700 in years 5 through 8. In actuality, you would continue to receive the $700 checks every year until the withdrawal account reached zero, which in this case, would take 14.2 years because of the 7% withdrawals. If the guarantee were only 5%, it would take 20 years to receive all of the original investment back, so the number of years depends on the percent of the guarantee. If you hadn't elected this rider, the contract would terminate in year 5 and that would be the end of it. Having elected the rider, however, even though the subaccounts you invested in severely under-performed and lost all of your investment; you would be guaranteed to receive your entire investment amount back through these yearly withdrawals.

Sounds like a good deal, right? Well, by now, I'm pretty sure you know what my answer is going to be! The answer is probably not for the majority of investors. The reason I say that is because VA con-tracts allow for a specific number of withdrawals every year, usually 10% of the contract value, to be withdrawn penalty free. Now, let's put a few more facts that we know together and see if this benefit is really worth the additional cost. Historically speaking, we know that the S&P 500 has returned over 10% per year on average. We also know that bond funds, which are more conservative investments than stocks because they invest primarily in government bonds and bonds issued by financially secure corporations, have historically returned on average about 6% to 7% per year. Finally, we also know that money market funds, which deal in cash instruments and are about the most conservative accounts an investor could possibly invest in, have historically had annual returns between 4% to 5%. Putting all that information together, let me ask you another question:

Do you, as an investor, even investing quite conservatively, reasonably expect to earn an average of 6% to 7% per year over the life of your investment?

If the answer is yes, and I can tell you that your answer should unequivocally be yes, then why would I need a rider such as this? You see, if you expect to earn 6% to 7% on average per year, and we assume you are taking withdrawals of somewhere between 5% and 7%, the percents offered on these riders by insurance companies, then your contract value would be staying relatively level. I say relatively level because in terms of subaccount performance some years will be better than others, but on average, your account is staying level at your initial investment. The doom and gloom scenario of your contract value declining to the point of it reaching $0 is extremely remote. Is it possible? Yes. Is it likely? Absolutely not. This again goes back to preying on investor's worst fears. The worst fear of any investor is that they're going to lose all their money. That should rightly be every common investor's greatest fear, because as common investors, we only have a limited amount of money to invest, and if we lose it, we fall into serious financial jeopardy. However, there is a difference between having a worst fear and allowing that fear to govern our rational decision-making process. The simple fact is that withdrawal benefits such as these are only beneficial if the contract value plummets rapidly in the first few years, and you, as the investor, know that for those years, you must have this designated stream of income guaranteed. Remember that the contract usually allows for 10% of contract value a year to be withdrawn penalty free, so if the contract value drops sharply in those first few years, that is when these types of benefits could be beneficial. In our above example, if we were simply taking regular withdrawals and didn't elect a withdrawal benefit rider, and we look at year 3, when our contract value has dropped from $10,000 to $5,000 our free withdrawal amount would only be $500 (10% of $5,000). Assuming we must have $700 per year, we take a $700 withdrawal but now that our contract value is only $5,000; that represents a 14% withdrawal, which would put us over our free withdrawal amount of 10% and we could incur surrender charges. Typically, the CDSC on a VA contract lasts between seven and nine years, but we will discuss that more in depth in the next section. So, in that scenario, the withdrawal benefit would be beneficial because the $700 would be guaranteed and not subject to CDSC even if it does exceed the 10% free withdrawal amount. But notice the sharp decline required for the benefit to really be useful. Our contract value would have to drop below $7,000 before the benefit would really pay dividends, because once the contract value drops below $7,000, the $700 withdrawal would constitute a greater then 10% withdrawal. That is a 30% decline in account value in the first few years of the contract, and if we have invested conservatively, that is highly unlikely. The reason I keep mentioning the first few years is that once your CDSC period is over, let's assume it's seven years, you can withdrawal as much from the contract as you see fit with no penalties. It would no longer matter that the $700 withdrawal was greater than 10% of your contract value because you no longer have any surrender charges left on the contract.

Allow me to touch on another point about these withdrawal benefits while we are talking about the CDSC on the VAs. These benefits can actually restrict your access to cash during your CDSC period, which we said is typically the first seven to nine years on most products. In most cases, our free withdrawal amount during the CDSC period is 10% of the contract value, higher than the 5% to 7% that the withdrawal benefit guarantees. Well, if you need to take a withdrawal over the 5% to 7% that this living rider guarantees, there are adverse consequences. Assume in the third year you need to take the full 10% withdrawal allowable under your contract, so you exceed the 5% to 7% guaranteed by the rider. The negative consequences associated with this could range from a reduction of the amount in your withdrawal account, thereby reducing the amount of future income you can receive, or in the most extreme case, it can result in the forfeiture of the rider altogether. In any of these cases, exceeding the guaranteed amount is not only detrimental to the future income stream you will be guaranteed, but also, it effectively limits your free withdrawal percentage from 10% of contract value down to between 5% to 7%. This is another factor to keep in mind when considering this type of living rider.

Summary of Living Benefits

As you have probably surmised by now, I'm not a big fan of living benefits such as the three we have discussed. I'm on record as saying that riders such as these prey on investors' worst fears in order to generate higher fees for insurance companies, and from my experience in the industry, this is the absolute truth. That doesn't mean investors should NEVER attach a living rider to their annuity contract, because there are very few things in this world that you can say you should NEVER do. There are certain cases and a select few investors whom these riders benefit because they give them peace of mind. Even though the peace of mind guarantees they receive are artificial in the sense that historical facts about investing and the stock market strongly suggest that none of these worst-case scenarios would ever come to fruition, it still puts their minds at ease. This is where knowing yourself and what kind of investor you are will determine which one, if any, of these living riders is suitable for you. The vast majority of you reading this book should not purchase a living rider on your VA. Here are a few questions to ask yourself, and by answering them, you can rather accurately determine if paying for a living rider is in your best interest:

1) *Can I, as an investor, live with periodic fluctuations in the market, both positive and negative, without overreacting to either one?*

2) *Am I the kind of investor who needs a peace-of-mind guarantee against a worst-case scenario, regardless of cost or practicality, in order to sleep at night?*

3) *Is this VA that I'm investing in going to be my primary source of income in retirement?*

4) *Do you, as an investor, want to retain control over your VA without having to annuitize and be able to decide when and how much of a withdrawal you need in any given year?*

The first two questions can help you determine the kind of investor you are generally. If the answer to the first question is no, and any kind of short-term fluctuations in the stock market at all make you nervous and worried, then perhaps you could consider a living rider. If you couple that answer of no to the first questions with a yes to the second question, then you can certainly move on to questions 3 and 4. That would mean that you are a pessimistic type of investor and are primarily concerned with the worst-case possibility that could come from a particular investment. I want to make clear here that this is neither good nor bad and not a judgment on my behalf at all. I'm not condemning anyone for thinking this way because it is your money and you have every right to have this type of outlook on any investment you make. This is simply trying to determine what kind of investor you are and what your risk tolerances are. If the answer to the first two questions are no and yes, in that order, that suggests you are a very risk-averse investor. You would probably hold most of your assets in government bonds, CDs, or cash, safe investments that have very specific rates of return. Falling into this investment group places you in the primary target market of insurance companies selling VAs with these types of living riders. Remember, I said the word "guarantee" doesn't get to be used by investment representatives very often, but it can be invoked in this case because the living riders are guaranteeing you something, and it puts your mind at ease as a risk-averse investor, even though the price and practicality of the riders aren't justified in most cases. They can talk to you about a 5% to 7% guarantee, whether it is an income benefit or a withdrawal benefit rider, and to investors in government bonds, CDs, or cash instruments that sounds like a very attractive offer. Especially since in today's market with interest rates as low as they are, these investments have very low yields. The ten-year US Treasury bond as of November 2004 is only yielding a rate of about 4.2%. CDs are generally in the same range or slightly higher and cash investments such as money markets or most savings accounts are paying less then 1%. More often than not, as I have touched on before, the riders are not properly explained to you, as the investor, because the investment representatives themselves often don't fully understand them. Being the target market for these types of products, it is so vitally important for you to understand them before you are pitched a sales idea and purchase something you don't need or can't use. The other major reason why you are the target market for these products deals with the commissions that investment representatives get paid. If you have your money with an investment representative of any brokerage firm in the country, or in the world for that matter, and you are investing primarily in government bonds, CDs, and money market funds, they are getting paid very little commission on those trades. In fact, if you're money is in cash or in a money market fund, they are lucky if they get paid any commission at all on those assets. Remember that they are commission-based sales people, just like any other sales force in any other industry, and the products they tend to sell are the highest commission-paying products! I can't tell you how many conversations on the phone I've had with investment representatives over the years that have gone very similar to this:

Me: "Well, Mr. Investment Rep, these are the products that you can sell to your clients..."
Mr. X: "Very good, now which one pays the higher commission?"

This is a cold hard fact. I know there are investment representatives who take strong personal stakes in their clients' futures and really do look out for their best interests, but the financial marketplace is filled with representatives who are in the business to earn high commissions and make six or seven figures a year and that is their primary concern. This might offend certain people in the financial community, but I really don't care. This is the fact, and you, as the common investor, deserve to know it.

Investment representatives don't get paid well on the cash instruments you as a risk-averse investor hold in your account. However, VAs pay generous commissions, as much as 7% to 8% upfront to the representative or slightly less up front, maybe 4% to 5% and pay them trail commissions. A trail commission is a residual commission generated to the representative from the original sale. An example would be if an investment representative sells a VA to a client and the initial investment is $100,000. The investment representative has a few different choices for how their commissions get paid to them. If they take the upfront option, the one that can pay 7% to 8%, we will say 7% for this example, they get a check for $7,000 for that sale and that is it. They receive no future compensation for that sale. If, however, they choose the trail option and take less upfront, we will say 5%, they would receive a check for the $5,000 at the time of the sale, and beginning the next year, they would receive another check for their trail commission. The trail commission is usually between .50% and 1.00%. In this case, it would most likely be .5% of the account value. That is an important point to keep in mind; the trail commissions they receive are based on the account value of your contract. As your contract value increases, so does their commission trail check. Since there is very little room for growth in just cash instruments, it provides the investment representative the opportunity to have that residual income grow over the years. So they can get paid roughly .10% to .20% on the assets they have under management in cash instruments, or they can get paid 5% upfront and receive .50% a year in commissions. Which would you choose? Obviously that is a rhetorical question, but it is a golden opportunity for the insurance companies and their wholesaling forces to convince investment representatives to place their clients in VAs.

One of the easiest and most effective sales pitches a wholesaler can make to an investment representative is this:

"Mr. Investment Rep, think of all the clients you have currently and what percent currently have money sitting on the sidelines in cash instruments? How much are you getting paid on that business? I can offer you a product with certain guarantees you can sell your clients on and not only double the amount of trails you're earning on those assets, but also give you an immediate upfront payout of 5%."

That's an easy sell. Investment representatives can convince themselves that VAs with these riders attached to them are the right thing for their clients and collect the checks. Remember back to our discussion of mutual funds and how A shares of mutual funds have breakpoints that lower the expense charge for purchasing the shares according to the dollar amount being invested? That is not the case with annuities. The same commission percent gets paid to the investment representative regardless of if it's a $10,000 investment or a $1,000,000 investment. This is yet another reason the sale of VAs has increased so rapidly over the last decade.

If you think that commissions don't factor into what is being sold to you, then you are doing yourself an injustice. Ask the investment representative what they are getting paid on the sale. They will most likely dance around the issue and say that it is really none of your concern what their commission is, but in my opinion, that is a load of crap. It is every bit your concern, and you have a right to know because you are the one they're soliciting business from! It's your money, your hard-earned money, and you have every right to know why they are pitching you this product. Is it because they believe it's suitable for you or because they're earning a large commission on the trade? The reason may be both, but understanding how investment representatives get paid is essential for you because it can give you great insight as to potential reasons of why you are being sold a given product.

Going back to our list of questions, if you answer no to the first question and yes to the second, then go ahead and look at questions 3 and 4. If you didn't answer that way to the first two questions, then there is no need for you to go on to questions 3 and 4 because a living rider is most likely not suitable for you. Assuming the answer to question 3 is yes and the VA is going to be your primary source of income in retirement and you absolutely can't afford to take any losses whatsoever, then a living benefit may be something you are willing to pay the extra expenses for. If you know you need that amount of money to generate a certain income stream because you have no other real assets from which to draw an income in retirement, then perhaps an income benefit may suit you. If that's not the case, and the VA is simply going to act as an occasional supplement to your retirement income, then there is no need to answer question 4 because you don't need to pay the extra fees for a living benefit.

We've now gone through the first three questions and determined that a living benefit might be a possibility for our situation, then the fourth question is the whole determining factor. A yes answer to this question in all likelihood means you don't want a living benefit. It means that retaining control over your VA and being able to determine the frequency and amount of income you need in any given year is important to you and the two living riders we discussed that deal with income, the income benefit and the withdrawal benefit, would hinder that ability. Either you would have to annuitize the contract and give up control to take advantage of the income benefit, or you would be limited in the amount you could withdrawal every year under the withdrawal benefit without jeopardizing the effectiveness of the rider. On the contrary, if you know for certain that ten or fifteen years down the line, you are going to need a designated fixed income stream, no more or no less, to aid you in retirement then a living rider could work for you. Honestly, how many of us know what we are going to need ten or fifteen years from now? Planning for retirement is exceedingly important; as I have emphasized in this book, it is probably one of the three or four biggest decisions we make in our lives, but it doesn't mean that we should pay higher expenses, sometimes drastically high, for features that don't give us much practical value in return. These living riders prey on our worst fears, and the sales forces of insurance companies are well trained in how to package them in a way that makes them seem necessary and practical when they really aren't. I know because I've been trained my entire career on how to position and sell them over the phone to investment representatives. Don't be fooled by the smoke-and-mirrors sales pitches that you will hear. Ask questions about what you are buying and before you purchase it, get at least a second opinion and probably a third opinion. Ask another investment representative, or better yet, ask me through my Website that is listed under my contact information in the book, and I'll gladly help you walk through the ins and outs of any annuity product. The vast majority of investors such as ourselves don't need these living benefits, but as

I've stated, there are instances where they could be appropriate and suitable but certainly not to the tune of the hundreds of billions of dollars being sold every year.

Tax Deferral

We've mentioned this in the course of our discussion so far, but it deserves further emphasis. I said that a VA is akin to a tax-deferred mutual fund with certain guarantees, whether they are during the owner's lifetime or upon their death, but the other primary reason for their popularity is their tax-deferred status. It allows them to take advantage of what is known as triple compounding. Triple compounding is the idea that money inside an annuity earns gains on not only the original investment, but also on the gains accumulated within the contract as well as on the money you have saved by not paying taxes every year. So, by not paying tax on the gains in the contract every year and reinvesting those gains, you earn that triple compounding effect.

Chapter 11 - What Does All This Cost?

We've touched on some of the costs associated with VAs, but now, let's put all those pieces together and see exactly how much we are going to be charged every year for this kind of investment. The base fee in any VA is called the mortality and expense charge (M&E), and it, in essence, pays for the death benefit provided by any given contract. The M&E expenses generally range from 1.25% to 1.75%, with a few falling above and below that range. The more extensive a death benefit that a contract has, for instance the step-up or roll-up features we discussed earlier, the higher the base M&E will be. In addition to the M&E charge, most insurance companies also charge an administrative charge to cover the costs of sending out quarterly statements, Website and phone services, and other miscellaneous administrative tasks associated with running their annuity business. This charge typically ranges between .10% and .20% per year and is tacked on to the M&E expense. So, with no living benefits attached to the VA and without factoring into account the costs associated with the subaccounts that we're going to invest in, we are looking at charges of anywhere from 1.35% to 1.95%. This is certainly not a cheap investment given what we know from our examination of how expenses can impact our returns.

One important point I want to note about the M&E expense is that the charge is not taken out of your account all at once, for instance on December 31st of every year, but rather, is taken on a daily basis. For example, if the M&E charge were 1.50%, that charge would be divided by 365 days and roughly .0041% would be deducted from your account value every day. This really accomplishes two important objectives for the insurance company in that the expense is spread out over the entire year, never leaving the investor one big fee to pay and that means the expense doesn't show on the investor's quarterly statement. You or I, as the investor, receive quarterly statements on our contract showing the current value and how it has performed over that time period, but the one thing on those statements that you won't see are the M&E charges because they are taken out daily. In essence, they are hidden charges because we never see the amount of the charges or how they impacted our contract value, we just see the performance numbers net of all fees. Some of the living riders can be charged in this manner, although most are charged on a quarterly basis which means those fees will show on the quarterly statement as having been deducted during that particular quarter. It is just something to keep in mind as to how the insurance companies charge for these contracts and why you won't see those charges on any statements you receive.

We now know the base charges that will come with our contract and pay for the death benefit, and for right now, we'll assume that we don't elect any living riders. The next expense to factor in is the expense of the subaccounts we are going to invest in. These expenses will range very similarly to the expenses of the retail mutual funds we talked about earlier. That chart we examined with the ranges of expenses you would be willing to pay would still be a good guide although we must take into account that the expenses of those funds inside of VAs are generally a few basis points higher then their retail counterparts. The subaccount expenses you pay are comprised of a weighted average of all the funds you choose. For example, if you chose to invest 50% into an index subaccount charging .50% and 50% into a large-cap growth subaccount charging 1.00% your sub-account expense would be .75%. So it's an average of which funds you invest in and how much you invest in each fund. In our example, let's assume we invest in a solid large-cap growth fund charging 1.00%. We couple this with our total M&E expense, which includes the administrative charge of 1.50%, and that gives us a total expense ratio of 2.50% per year on our VA contract. Knowing what you now know of how important expenses are in determining future performance, you can see that this is a hefty price to pay. However, you are getting the two important benefits of tax-deferred growth and a guaranteed death benefit payout to your beneficiaries. The question now becomes:

"What are my goals for this investment?"

If the ultimate goal is to pass on money to your heirs, then this is probably a very suitable investment because it will allow that money to grow at a quicker rate due to the nature of tax-deferral and if you were to pass away at a time when the market is struggling and the value of your investment had fallen, you would know there would be a guarantee in place for those beneficiaries. Shopping around for a low-cost VA, however, is still vitally important because a difference of just 15 or 20 basis points per year in expenses over 10 or 20 years can costs you tens of thousands or even hundreds of thousands of dollars in lost performance gains. This is the niche that VAs are most suitable for in my opinion. People who can't get underwritten for life insurance or just don't want to go through the process can still invest in a tax-deferred vehicle that will guarantee a legacy to their heirs. Annuities can provide a stream of income to retirees, but in most cases, investors such as you or I don't want to give up control of our contract by annuitizing, and as we've examined, in most cases, it's more beneficial to simply take withdrawals from the contract when needed then to annuitize.

Surrender Charges

We've touched on these expenses briefly, but for the most part, they work very much like the CDSC on the back end of B-share mutual funds. Let's take another look at that table to refresh our memories:

Year	CDSC%
1	6%
2	5%
3	4%
4	4%
5	3%
6	3%
7	2%
8	1%

The schedule for a VA will vary slightly from this model; most are seven-year schedules versus eight-year, and they will tend to be more heavily front-loaded. By front-loaded, I mean the first few years will usually be higher, around 7% or 8% instead of 6%. Again, these schedules vary from product to product and company to company. There are VA products on the market that have CDSC schedules as short as three years and as long as nine years. There are also VAs on the market now that have no CDSC schedule at all, meaning that two days after you purchase the contract, you could withdrawal all of your money with no penalty. Now the M&E on these products is substantially higher then on other VA contracts in order to compensate for that enhanced liquidity so there is a trade-off. The point I want to emphasize here as well is that the length of the CDSC will also determine M&E charges associated with the contract. The shorter the CDSC schedule, the higher the M&E will be. What the insurance company is basically telling you is that by having a shorter CDSC schedule, meaning you could take all your money away from us penalty-free in let's say three years versus seven years, we are going to charge you higher annual expenses in order to compensate for that. The surrender charges are in place to offset the cost of the annuity and help to keep the pricing of the product as low as possible. The reason the insurance company can charge an M&E charge of only 1.25% for a seven-year basic death benefit VA is that they know if you leave before your CDSC schedule is over, they will recoup those expenses on the back end through those surrender charges. The actuaries working for the insurance companies have priced the product to be profitable, and they know that if you leave the majority of those assets with the company for the full seven years, then through the M&E charges and the ability of the company to reinvest those fees to further grow the company, they will have made a handsome profit from your contract. Once the CDSC schedule is over, the insurance company has already made their profit and you are free to withdraw your money penalty-free or leave it there; it is up to you.

The CDSC schedule only comes in to play if we, as investors, exceed our free withdrawal amount during that time. I touched on this earlier, but in most VA contracts, the investor can withdrawal up to 10% of the contract value each year without incurring any form of surrender penalty. For example, we invest $10,000 into a VA, and if we needed to take a withdrawal, we would have access to 10%, which would work out to roughly $1,000. I say roughly because if the contract states that we have access to 10% of the contract value then that $1,000 could fluctuate depending on whether the account was up or down. If the contract had risen to $11,000 when we requested the 10% withdrawal, we would receive $1,100, and on the flip side of that equation, if the contract value had fallen to $9,000 at the time of the withdrawal, we would only have access to $900. That is an important aspect to keep in mind when considering taking a withdrawal. There are still a few VAs on the market that allow investors to take 10% of the original investment premium, meaning the investor could take 10% of the original $10,000 regardless of the contract value at the time. Most of these have gone out of favor because it limits the investor to the dollar amount they can withdrawal if their account is rising. If the account grows to $15,000, they are still restricted to 10% of the original $10,000, and most investors weren't pleased with this type of feature. It's only human nature to want to have greater access to your cash as your investment grows. But as you can see, the downside to taking 10% of the contract value occurs when the contract has had some losses, taking it below the initial premium amount and thus reducing the dollar amount the investor could take as a withdrawal.

Once the CDSC schedule is over, then the investor has access to 100% of the remaining contract value with no penalties. That is one of my main arguments against living benefits that require you to annuitize to take advantage of them, because you are already 100% liquid in your contract by that time and can take periodic withdrawals as your needs dictate and not be forced to essentially end your contract with no ability for future growth and give control of those withdrawals over to the insurance company and be forced to take a set withdrawal every year whether you need it or not. If you need more than that annuity payment, you can't access it because you've given up control of that asset!

One last point about taking withdrawals from your VA contract that I want to share with you is that there is an IRS-imposed 10% penalty for withdrawals made prior to the owner reaching the age of 59 ½. This is one of the restrictions imposed on taking withdrawals from annuities because they enjoy a tax-deferred status. The IRS allows the investment to grow tax-deferred, but in exchange for that, they want control over when the investor has access to those gains without paying a penalty. Basically, the 59 ½ rule is in place to discourage investors from trying to manipulate the system by using tax-deferred vehicles to skate around paying taxes to the government. For instance, an investor who is thirty-five and looking for means to invest without incurring a tax bill every year can use a VA but must not withdrawal any of the gains in that VA contract over the next twenty-five years until they reach 59 ½ or be forced to pay that premature distribution penalty to the IRS. For investors close to retirement or already in retirement, this probably isn't as much of an issue because most are already nearing 59 ½ or have already passed that age so the point is moot. However, it's an important rule that we, as investors, need to be aware of because it can impact our ability to access the money within our contract. Now this 10% penalty only applies to the GAINS within the contract and not to the original premium (unless the contract is an IRA or other type of qualified retirement account, then the entire amount may be subject) so if the VA has no gains or has incurred some losses, then this penalty may very well not apply. There are, of course, exceptions that the IRS grants, but there is no need to get in depth with all those options now. If you have more detailed questions, I would recommend speaking with a tax attorney or tax accountant or logging on to www.irs.gov and browsing through their Website which has links to frequently asked questions on this subject. That should be able to answer most of your questions.

Premium Bonus

One other additional feature and expense that VAs can offer is a premium bonus. Some products have a bonus feature built into them and some have it as an optional feature that can be selected when the product is purchased. In essence, it gives the investor an immediate cash bonus on their initial investment, and in some cases, subsequent payments as well. For example, let's say we purchase a VA with a built-in bonus feature (these products are referred to as bonus products) for an initial investment of $10,000. That investment of $10,000 is automatically credited with a bonus, usually between 4% and 6%, immediately and gets invested into the subaccounts. We'll assume a 5% bonus on our $10,000 means that instead of just $10,000 being invested, $10,500 gets invested for us. The insurance company, in essence, just placed an additional $500 into our account. Since this is a bonus product, it means that if we make any future payments into the contract, they will also get credited that bonus.

If you've been reading carefully, and I'm sure you have, then I know exactly what you're thinking right about now:

"What's the catch?"

Great question! The catch is that a product such as this will pay for that bonus somehow. As I'm sure you know by now, insurance companies aren't in the business of just giving away free money! I can't blame them; any business that is going to just give out money with no strings attached isn't going to be in business for long. In exchange for the bonus, the insurance company will either add years onto the CDSC schedule, increase the M&E expense slightly, or pay out a lower commission to the investment representative. It could also be a combination of all three methods! Bonus products were quite the rage in the late 1990s when they first got introduced to the marketplace because it was a great way for investment representatives to move their clients from one product to another and offset any surrender penalties the client might have incurred. For example, an investment representative sells an existing client on the new bonus product paying a 5% bonus and transfers the client's money from one insurance company to another. In this scenario, we'll assume the client still had a CDSC of 3% they had to pay to the original issuing company when they transferred the money out, so the sale is that the 5% bonus on the new product will offset the 3% CDSC they're getting charged. The client only gets a slight increase in their contract value and starts a brand new CDSC schedule, most likely eight years or longer, but the investment representative gets paid a brand new commission. So who made out on that deal? The investment representative gets paid another 5% to 7% while only giving the client at best a 2% increased contract value and starting their surrender charge schedule all over again. You can see now why it was such an effective sales tool. The investment representative could now justify moving their client's money around every few years and keep receiving those commissions with every transaction. Well, suitability regulations, some imposed by the states and the NASD and some imposed by investment firms themselves, have curbed the use of this practice, but it still exists today.

Keep this in mind when offered a bonus product, because trust me that you're paying for it in one way or another. I'm not going to make a blanket statement and say you should never choose a bonus on a product, but remember that a voice should go off in your head and remind you to ask detailed questions if the subject comes up. Ask questions such as:

1) *Do my M&E expenses go up?*

2) *How long is the CDSC schedule if I choose the bonus?*

3) *Can the insurance company take the bonus back for any reason?*

Gathering this key information will greatly assist you in weighing your options and deciding whether the bonus is in your best interests or not.

<u>*Summary*</u>

Now, that is quite a bit of information on VAs that we just covered. It may take reading this section more then once before all of the concepts I touched on really start to become clear. Remember, the goal here is to grasp the fundamentals of VAs and the different options available on them so you can ask the right questions. Annuities, particularly VAs, can be complex investment vehicles with enough intricacies and tax regulations surrounding them that it is virtually impossible for the common investor to know them in depth. I've been working with annuities of all kinds for the last five years, and I admit that I don't know all there is to know about every annuity, that's how complex they can be. That shouldn't make you apprehensive about investing in annuities, just make sure you do your homework and get more then one opinion before investing in one.

Section IV - Fixed Annuities

This is the second of our categories of annuities and is the easiest to fully grasp. A fixed annuity, unlike the VAs we have been discussing, returns to the investor a guaranteed rate over the term of the contract. The rate is determined at purchase and never changes for the duration of the contract. In this way, it works very much like a tax-deferred CD. For instance, a ten-year fixed annuity might be yielding 5%, meaning that it will grow 5% a year compounding and growing tax-deferred. There are no market fluctuations, it never shows a loss on a statement, and it is a very conservative investment along the lines of a CD. CDs tend to offer higher rates because they are taxable investments, so to compensate for that, the rates are typically a little higher.

The same general rules apply to fixed annuities as apply to VAs in that they will have a surrender charge schedule, you can annuitize them and turn them into a stream of income payments, and as we already mentioned, they also grow tax-deferred. Banking institutions are typically the ones who sell the most fixed annuities because their client base tends to be the most conservative and can understand these products more easily because of their similarity to the CDs they've been investing in for many years. It's an easy sell for investment representatives at the bank and nets them a better commission then simply selling a CD. While the gross commissions tend to be around 3% for these products, which is significantly less then VAs, it is still greater then any payout a CD would yield to them.

There is no M&E expense associated with these products because there is no guaranteed death benefit; it simply is your contract value upon your death that is paid to your beneficiary. Since there is no chance for market fluctuation because you're not invested in any subaccounts, there is nothing for the insurance company to guarantee. They've already gone into the market and purchased the bonds to guarantee the rate they're paying you every year, so there is no real risk for them. The insurance company determines the rates on these products based on the prevailing rates in the marketplace. They typically buy government securities that match the duration of the annuity, in this case, let's say ten years, and let's assume the rate is 5%, then the actuaries factor in a profit margin, and you, as the investor, will probably be offered a rate somewhere in that general range.

That, in a nutshell, is fixed annuities. They're not terribly popular investment vehicles right now because interest rates at this time are at all-time lows. However, when rates start to exceed that 5% range and start pushing up near 6% or 7%, then insurance companies start writing quite a bit of fixed business because, as I said, it's an easy sell for the investment representative. A straightforward product with a solid, guaranteed rate of return is usually a slam-dunk sale for any investment representative.

My personal thoughts on fixed annuities are that when rates are up around the 6% to 7% range, they can be a viable alternative to CDs for a portion of your money. It defers some of that tax burden and is a very safe and cheap alternative way for you to grow your money and annuitize in the future if that is your long-term goal. If rates are as low as they are now, I would stay away from fixed-rate products such as these because you don't want to lock your money up for the long term when rates are low. Rates have been at an all-time low for the past two years and really have nowhere to go but up. However, if you lock yourself into a five-year or longer investment at say 4% today, and rates start rising as they are now, then in a year or two when rates are back over 5%, you'll be kicking yourself. As a general rule, don't invest in long-term fixed-rate products when rates are low, it will only hurt you in the long-term. I said they're good for a portion of your money because remember, they do still have a CDSC schedule and that will limit the amount of money you can access from them every year, so certainly don't tie up the majority of your assets in them.

Section V - Index Annuities

The last category of annuities I had on the list was index annuities. They are somewhat of a hybrid between variable and fixed
annuities. In most cases, they have several moving parts and can be
quite complex, but in their most basic form, your money is indexed to
the performance of an index, usually the S&P 500, and if that index
rises, then your account value rises. That sums them up in a rather
simplistic way, but I don't want to overwhelm you with detail.

Generally speaking, they don't have an M&E charge attached
to them. However, they can have exceedingly long and oppressive
CDSC schedules, sometimes as high as 15% to 20% and lasting for
longer than ten years. The reason for those excessive CDSC charges
is to pay for the commission payouts to the investment representatives, which in some cases, can be as high as 10% to 12%! That
is a HUGE payout to brokers and is oftentimes enough reason by
itself for them to sell such products. That is not all index annuities;
there are some on the market that charge no M&E and have CDSC

schedules more closely resembling the surrender charges associated with VAs.

These products generally have a minimum floor that the account value will rise by every year regardless of how well the index performs. For example, if the index declines by 5% in any year, your contract value would still rise by a certain percentage, usually around 3%. So it has some downside protection. However, there is a trade-off for that downside protection. They also have limits on how much you can earn in any particular year. Continuing with our example, let's assume the index had a good year and was up 15%, you would be capped as to how much of that gain you would receive. In most cases, the cap would be around 7%, meaning that you would only realize a gain of 7% even though the index gained 15%. How the insurance companies calculate the gains of the index can vary, and in some cases, be slightly complicated, but generally, there are two methods:

1) <u>Monthly Averaging</u>—In this scenario, the company takes the monthly value of the index for all twelve months of the year and averages them out. They then compare that average number to the value of the index when your contract started, and that is the percent increase or decline. This method helps to smooth out any drastic swings that might take place in the index during the year. One really bad month won't have as great of a negative impact because the better performing months can offset it. On the flip side of that is that one really fantastic month of performance can also be offset by the poorly performing months. So, if the difference between the average gain of the index for the year and the starting value of the index at the beginning of the contract year was 10%, your account would get credited 7% because of the cap.

2) <u>Point-to-Point</u>—This calculation method doesn't use any averaging but rather looks at the value of the index at the start of the contract year and the value of the index

on the final day of that year. This is riskier than monthly averaging because if that final month is a sharp decline for the index, then it can cost you any gains for that year. On the other hand, it can be beneficial if that final month shows stellar performance for the index. With greater risk comes greater reward, and generally, with point-to-point calculations the caps are higher, allowing you to take part in a greater portion of the earnings in the index.

Index annuities can be a very viable alternative for investors interested in fixed annuities or CDs because of the downside protection, but they can also give the investor the ability to participate in the gains of the market. This can help in outpacing the rise of inflation, which is always a concern for conservative investors. However, it is an absolute imperative that you, as the investor, do your homework on these products! If you get sold the wrong one and get locked into one of those long, oppressive CDSC schedules I mentioned earlier, it is going to be a stiff penalty for you to ever get out of that contract.

A general rule of thumb what I would suggest for these products would be to look for one that doesn't have an M&E charge and has a surrender charge schedule of no greater then seven to nine years and doesn't exceed 8% in any of those years. The calculation methods as well as the caps and minimum guarantees will vary from product to product, and you need to choose ones that you are comfortable with.

Section VI - The Bottom Line

We've covered quite a bit of information, but believe me, we have really just scratched the surface. Mutual funds and annuities can certainly be more complex than simply what we've tackled in this book. However, after reading this, you'll be armed with the fundamentals you'll need to help make sense of any such investment proposed to you. You always hear coaches in sports stressing the importance of fundamentals, and how most games are won or lost based on which team does the little things, the fundamental things correctly. We even hear this mantra from CEOs of corporations throughout the world, except they refer to concentrating on the company's core competencies. Core competencies is corporate lingo for a company focusing on the fundamentals that built the company and keeping those basic concepts in focus as they attempt to grow their business. Investing is the same way: stay focused on the fundamentals of diversification and being consistent through up markets and down markets, and your money will grow over time.

The primary reason why I wrote this book was to educate common investors about some of the main reasons why investing in mutual funds and annuities can be advantageous and also to warn against a few of the pitfalls that await when investing in these products. You now have the knowledge to decipher for yourself whether a particular investment is suitable for your needs and are no longer reliant solely on the advice of your investment representative or pundits you may see on TV. One of my biggest fears is that investors in the marketplace are basing too many of their decisions on information they hear on financial shows aired on both TV and radio. Don't let opinions you hear on these shows jade your view on certain investments, because despite the credentials of these individuals, their opinions are all too often biased and uninformed. The opinions offered on these shows often lean towards one extreme or another. For instance, they either have a disdain for annuities and believe them to be over-priced, unsuitable investments for anyone, or they are on the other extreme and advocate annuities as investment vehicles that everyone should invest in. In actuality, neither opinion is correct. Those opinions are designed to be controversial and drive ratings. Anyone who simply dismisses annuities offhand is taking an ignorant point of view and the flip side is also correct for anyone advocating the suitability of annuities for all investors. The truth lies somewhere in the middle. I can't stress enough how important it is for common investors such as ourselves to gather multiple opinions before making an investment decision. Don't let just one person or group of people sell you anything until you have done some homework on the subject and consulted another investment representative or financial professional about it. Do you buy a car without shopping around from dealership to dealership in order to gather information and find the best terms for your investment? Of course not. I'll emphasize once again that investment representatives are some of the most highly skilled and well-trained salesmen (and women) in the world. In order to be successful in their field, they must not only be proficient in prospecting new clients but closing those new clients and getting them to buy their idea. Please keep this in mind when considering making any investment.

I think I've made my feelings on mutual funds and annuities pretty clear throughout the course of this book, but it certainly deserves further emphasis. Mutual funds and annuities are good investments and are important tools to use in wealth accumulation and retirement planning. That is as plain as I can make it. At times, I may have sounded cynical to the nature of the investment world, and that's because there are areas of the financial world that are objectionable, but the majority of companies and individuals involved in investing your money are forthright and trustworthy. These money managers and financial professionals are the best at what they do and, as I've stated before, are among the brightest minds in the world. Investors need to leverage that expertise and take full advantage of the benefits it can reap. However, selecting the means by which to do so is really an important choice for the investor. Choosing the right mutual fund or mutual funds as well as choosing the proper annuity with the proper features to fit your needs is where the information you've just learned can be put to use.

Everyone in the financial community agrees that mutual funds are good investments because they allow the investor to invest in the stock market by utilizing the expertise of the fund manager as well as allowing the investor to achieve adequate diversification with a rather small investment. Annuities, on the other hand, are a much more heated debate. I want everyone to read this next statement:

Annuities are GOOD investment vehicles!

This is a true statement coming from someone that has worked with annuities my entire career, and anyone who disagrees with this statement simply doesn't know what they are talking about. Now, I didn't say that ALL annuities are good investment vehicles, and I didn't say that ALL investors are suitable for annuities either. The concept of annuities as a way to either generate a stream of income in retirement or to provide an alternative to life insurance to guarantee a certain amount of assets to pass onto an investor's beneficiaries is a solid financial strategy. That is a fact. A certain percent of a certain investor's assets can definitely benefit from a tax-deferred investment such as an annuity. As we have talked about in some depth throughout this book, finding the right annuity at the right price with the right benefits is the challenge. I believe that annuities absolutely have their place in the portfolios of some investors for a certain portion of their assets. Do I believe that annuities should hold the majority of an investor's assets? In most cases, I would say no.

That was an overall perspective of annuities and mutual funds. Now, let me just sum up my point of view on some of the more specific topics we covered. Regarding mutual funds, remember to keep the following questions in mind:

1) *What are the total expenses charged for the fund?*

2) *How has the fund performed against its competition, particularly its Lipper peer group?*

3) *What sort of tax consequences can I expect from this particular fund? Is it going to pay out a high percent of dividends every year and does it have built-up capital gains liabilities in it?*

4) *Does this type of fund and how it's managed fit my particular risk tolerance?*

All of the above questions are important to consider, but I would stress questions 1 and 4. We've discussed and seen examples of the impact that expenses can have on our returns in terms of total dollars over a long investment period. The difference of just 0.2% can equate to tens of thousands or even hundreds of thousands of dollars over a ten, twenty, or thirty-year time horizon. Shop around for the best money manager at the best price. Please don't fall into the trap of thinking that 10 or 20 basis points really isn't that much of a difference, because in the long-term, and that's what most common investors are investing for, it can make a huge difference in the amount of money ending up in your wallet.

The final question doesn't have a straightforward answer unfortunately. I know I've alluded to this before, and I don't want to beat a dead horse, but the best asset an investor can have is to know themselves and their own risk tolerances. If we, as investors, can come to grips with the amount of volatility we're willing to accept in our investments, then it narrows our choices down significantly and opens the door for a much easier investment selection process. It's something you have to decide for yourself, or with the help of a good and trusted investment representative who can help you compile an accurate investment profile for yourself. Once armed with that knowledge and the information you've gathered in this book and from other material, you will be well on your way to making sound investment decisions.

Annuities, as we've learned, are a wholly different and unique animal. They can offer the tempting prospects of "guarantees" and other features that sound wonderful on the surface, but can be mind-numbingly useless and expensive when examined further. Let's first take a review of the death benefits associated with annuities, in particular, variable annuities. They are, in my opinion, the best feature about any annuity and should be the primary driving factor behind most annuity purchases. I'll go on record as saying that death benefits are very useful because they offer the investor a guarantee against the one inevitable factor of life, and that is death. Yes, as disturbing as it sounds or however unpleasant a thought it is, the fact still remains that all of us, at some point, are going to die. The other truth that accompanies this is that none of us know exactly when we are going to die. The death benefit in an annuity, just like the proceeds of a life insurance policy, can guarantee a known, set amount that will pass to our heirs regardless of when we die. The major difference being that life insurance proceeds pass tax-free while annuity earnings only pass tax-deferred. The step-up and roll-up features of VA death benefits that we discussed can guarantee certain dollar amounts that will be paid out to the beneficiary upon the owner's death despite how turbulent the stock market may be at the time. For example, in the late 1990s, many investors saw their IRAs, Individual Retirement Accounts, double or even triple in value due to the stock market explosion and the fantastic returns that mutual funds posted during these years. As we know, a large portion of those gains were then subsequently lost from the second half of 2000 through the end of 2002. If an investor would have had some of those assets invested in an annuity within their IRA and not solely in mutual funds, and they had the untimely misfortune of dying in 2002, then some of those gains would have been guaranteed to pass to their heirs through these death benefits. Since mutual funds simply pay out the contract value at the time of death in an IRA, there was no protection of those gains for many investors and those tremendous profits simply disappeared. This is an argument against one of the great myths of annuities, and that is the notion that annuities should NEVER be purchased to fund an investor's IRA. The reason given is that the IRA already enjoys tax-deferred status from the IRS so it makes no sense to place a tax-deferred investment inside an already tax-deferred vehicle. Simply point out the example we just ran through to anyone who is espousing this myth to you. I'm not saying that all IRAs should invest in annuities; however, IRAs with tremendous growth and earnings within them might consider placing a portion of those assets into an annuity to "lock-in" those gains for their heirs. By that I mean, no matter what happens to the rest of the assets in the IRA, and we'll assume all the other investments fall to $0, you as investors know that your beneficiaries, most likely your children, will have a guaranteed amount payable to them upon your death. The key to this, of course, as we know, is finding the right death benefit to suit your needs at the right M&E price.

This brings us back to our favorite subject of living benefits. I'm not a fan of living benefits; I never have been and I never will be. In isolated incidents, I think they can serve a purpose, but there is no justification for them being sold as prevalently in the marketplace as they are currently. Please remember what I've tried to emphasize to you in the course of this book, these living benefits sound fantastic when they are wrapped up and packaged in a slick, fancy sales pitch, but they are simply preying on your worst fears. They will promise you "guarantees" the vast majority of the time you don't need or won't ever use. The fees associated with them can be quite high, sometimes excessively so, and are simply ways for insurance companies to make their annuities seem more attractive and make them wildly more profitable.

Finally, we touched on fixed and index annuities. Fixed annuities work primarily the same way as CDs in that they guarantee an interest rate for a specified time period. However, the tax-deferred nature of the fixed annuities can make them a more attractive investment for certain investors. Index annuities, on the other hand, you need to be more careful with when considering as investments due to the excessively high surrender charges that can be associated with them. As I said previously, there are index annuities out on the market that are good investments, but there are also companies selling products that pay exceptionally high commissions to the investment representatives selling them and pay for these commissions by saddling the investor with longer and costlier surrender penalties. The one question you as an investor absolutely need to ask in regard to index annuities, along with the four questions I gave you earlier, is: What are the CDSC penalties associated with this product?

My goal in this book was to impart some of my knowledge of the inner workings of mutual funds and annuities from my career in the industry so that everyday investors would be properly equipped to make sound decisions. There is a great deal of detailed information I didn't include in this book, particularly regarding annuities, but quite frankly, it is knowledge only really gained from years of working in the industry and isn't necessary for all investors to know. It would become far too complicated and cumbersome for someone outside of the financial industry to know every detail pertaining to every benefit that different insurance companies offer and the tax ramifications of each. That's what investment professionals, CPAs, and tax attorneys are for. What the common investor does need to know, however, are the fundamentals of how these products work, and more importantly, why they are being sold to you. That question of why is quite powerful in all areas of life, and financial services are no different. It cuts through and clarifies whether or not an investment or a benefit offered on an investment is right for a particular investor. The questions of how and what are really just scenery to make the sales pitch and often obscure the real question of why. Why is this investment being sold to me? Why should I purchase it? Why is the insurance company offering me this "guarantee"? Why do I need it?

These are the questions that will reveal the truth about the different investment choices offered to you and aid you in your search to find the right one. I wish I could give you a list of every mutual fund and every annuity that I believe are the right investments and which are the wrong investments. Unfortunately, as I've said time and time again, it really is different and unique for every investor. No two investors are the same, and no two situations are exactly the same. All you can do is educate yourself as much as possible and then apply that knowledge to what is being presented to you. I hope I've helped you along that path and provided you with some insights into these products that you didn't previously have. I greatly appreciate you taking the time to read my book, and I sincerely hope that it aids you in your investment decisions. Thank you.

Notes and Resources

1) http://www.sec.gov

2) http://www.research.lipper.wallst.com

3) http://www.morningstar.com

4) http://www.savewealth.com

5) http://moneycentral.msn.com

6) http://www.nasd.com

7) http://www.navanet.org

About the Author

Jim McClelland is an experienced professional in the insurance industry. He has a B.S. in Finance from DeSales University as well as an MBA from the University of Notre Dame with concentrations in Finance and Management with over five years of experience with two of the leading insurance companies in the world selling and marketing mutual funds and annuities. He is an expert on both types of investments. His first-hand knowledge of the insurance sales marketplace gives him a unique insight to provide every reader with important questions to ask when considering a mutual fund or annuity purchase and certain sales tactics to be aware of.

If you would like to contact Jim please send an email to: annuityguru@comcast.net.